Memoirs of

TEACHING: THE GOOD, THE BAD AND THE INAPPROPRIATE

with strategies for teaching to children not to tests

CATHERINE IACCARINO

ISBN-10: 1479305200
ISBN-13: 9781479305209
LCCN: 2012917232

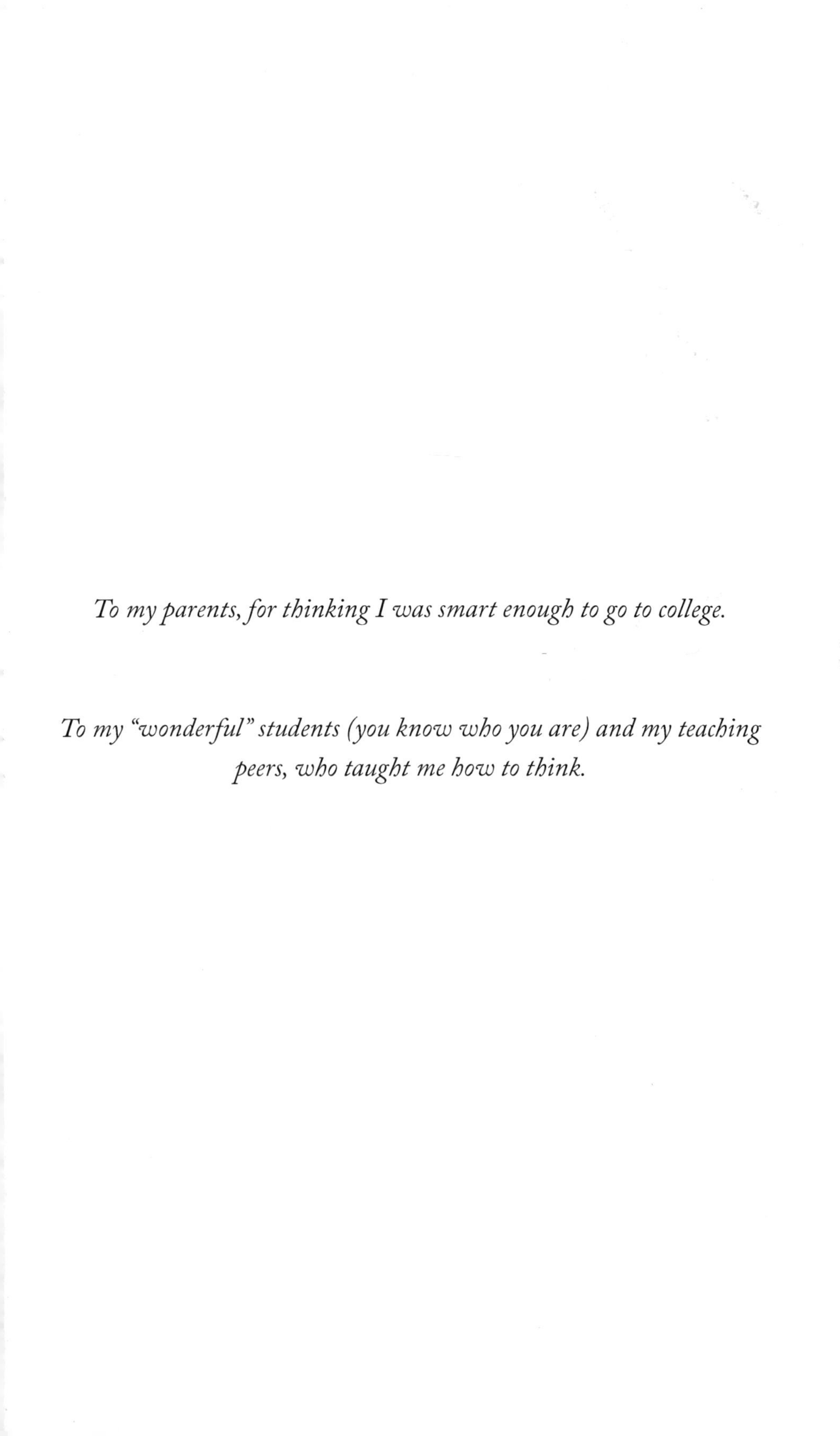

To my parents, for thinking I was smart enough to go to college.

To my "wonderful" students (you know who you are) and my teaching peers, who taught me how to think.

Contents

Part V
The Roll Models

Section 2/Strategies

Part VI
Departing From the Text

Part VII
It's all in the Presentation

INTRODUCTION

In the Beginning

I was a special-education resource room/inclusion teacher from January 1972 to June 2003. I taught mostly in grammar school, with some time at middle school. The last nine-plus years have been donated to many things, one of them was substitute teaching, mostly for the benefits. That adds up to quite a few years, which I'll leave you to count, and a lot of changes—some for the good, some for the bad ...and there's always the inappropriate. I learned a lot during that time teaching in a city of lower- to middle-income families. I live in the city myself; so along with it being a place with some major issues, it also has some major wonderful things about it, (including me). There's your first taste of my use of the sixth sense. Not the psychic sense kind, but one of the most important senses a teacher can have: the sense of humor. All teachers, like comedians, know that in order to keep their jobs and their sanity, they have to have a strong handle on that famous sixth sense. My sense of humor leans toward the sarcastic, tongue-in-cheek kind, even at my own expense. I like to be fair.

Now as I meander from school to school subbing, I've become reacquainted with many of my peers. From them and teachers from other districts I've stayed friends with,; I keep hearing the same chant-like lament. The sadness of missing what was once considered a standard procedure can be heard in their voices as they reminisce about the days gone by when there was time and freedom given to actually teaching. Teachers have become "Facilitators of mandates." Those aren't their exact words, but I like the title because with that many syllables they should be up for a pay raise. It might help with the rather dour mood that comes with the new territory. Plowing through piles of papers doesn't give as much joy as actually teaching. *Joy* is a very important one-syllable, three-letter word. Joy keeps the kids and the teachers working together on a common ground, and is a high motivator of learning. It seems teaching now has less to do with learning experiences and more to do with the correct vernacular when documenting the specific requirements of all those directives. The impetus for all this required record keeping seems due to the joyless emphasis has gone from teaching children to teaching to "the" test.

Many of my conversations with other teachers took place in the staff room over lunch. In some I participated, while others I used my highly tuned eavesdropping skills to ascertain. In keeping with the situation, I thought it only appropriate to conjure up a food analogy of the state of affairs: Visualize a banquet. Each course of food represents an academic skill or, an academic "course." All the guests (the students) are sitting around the table. In front of each one is a plate with exactly the same amount of food of exactly the same kind of food, all cooked up in exactly the same way. The teacher is not the chef. The teacher is the wait staff responsible for running around the table with fork in hand cramming the food (knowledge) down the guests' throats without allowing them to chew, taste, or digest each savory bite. Did I mention that the teacher, while frantically feeding each child, has one hand tied behind their back with a huge piece of red tape? At the end of the allotted dining time, the exhausted server gets to sit and the guests are full. Just don't ask them to remember what they ate, why they ate it, or if they enjoyed it. It would seem that education has become as processed as the food served up in the cafeterias. We all know how hard that can be to swallow.

So, what was it like before? What has changed? Who are some of these laws really protecting? What's being left out now and what's been added? What makes teachers and what we've learned from them memorable? What makes a student memorable, and how do students affect our teaching? What should we really be focusing on in teaching and how do we get that across? How do we get the "fun" back into the fundamentals of education? I ask myself these questions all the time. Well, that might be a slight exaggeration. But they have popped up on quite a few occasions. So I have tried in the pages that follow to answer these questions by reminiscing on my experiences, giving some comments and relatively easy ideas for teaching skills differently. Remember, I'm not saying these are the *only* answers or maybe always the *right* answers; they're just mine.

You may be asking, right about now, "What makes her think she has anything valuable to say or has better ideas about teaching?" Good question …it deserves an answer. For one thing, I'm old enough to have experienced all the changes and young enough to still remember them. I also had the exceptional opportunity to be a resource room teacher. This allowed me to work with small groups of students from kindergarten through fifth grade. I could experiment. I could modify. I could observe how they learned. I could draw conclusions. I could see what worked. I could also build a trusting relationship and a deeper level of communication. These things are close to impossible for classroom teachers to do. They are too busy focusing on curriculum mandates, huge divergences in skill level, and the sheer volume of students sitting before them. Last, but not least, I know what it's like to be learning disabled, and there's nothing like firsthand knowledge. If that's not enough, I had many years and just as many opportunities through subbing in regular education classrooms to try everything out in the classroom from first grade on up through middle school.

I have left out names or changed them to protect the innocent and me, of course. I have left out the race or religion of a child or teacher unless it is specifically relevant to the topic. I also left out so many other things I wanted to write about, but I didn't want this to be a saga or an instructional manual for some mastery test. Finally, I left out everything I did wrong and the kids I failed to reach. That's for another book. I did weave throughtout the book that sixth sense of humor, for the sake of sanity, of course. So when you read it, you might commiserate, be enlightened, feel justified, or find parts of it helpful in teaching. You might think it insipid and skip chapters. It's all up to you. There's no pressure coming from here. Just think of it as a buffet and take as much or as little as you want. I just hope you enjoy the menu.

Bon Appetit!

SECTION 1

MEMOIRS

PART 1

The Flair of the Faux Pas

*

You know what they say about the best-laid plans.
Truth be told (as it should be), sometimes the unexpected—verging on the social blunder—is the most enlightening, startling, or educationally enhancing experience.

1
Say What?

Halloween Music

A *stress test* is where you hop on a treadmill all hooked up to monitors and run, sweat, breathe heavy, and pray that your heart is all right. Then there is *test stress*, where you sit slumped and frozen in a chair, sweating, breathing heavy, and praying your answers are all right. A word of advice: never take a stress test after test stress— unless you have some serious masochistic tendencies. Then go for it.

It is painful to watch a child with test stress …the pen or pencil so tightly gripped in the hand that the child's knuckles are white. Other symptoms that may occur are lip biting, squinting, crinkling of the brow, and leg swinging. I think test stress is a major cause of children getting lower scores than they should. It just isn't fair, really. They studied, they learned, they did what was required, but the test is that one-eyed monster that lies across the desk and makes things go bump in their brains. And fear obstructs the retrieval of knowledge.

I tried to think of how to lower student stress levels and began by examining what *I* would use. I thought of obsessively playing solitaire on the computer. On further thought, I realized it was rather mind-numbing and required expensive equipment, not to mention that it promoted carpal tunnel. Maybe that was not the way to go. Next I came up with yoga, which I love. All that stretching is great. Of course, I wasn't about to engage the students in downward-facing dog or warrior poses. It would have been too difficult for them and embarrassing for me. I could, however, do my favorite parts beginning and ending with closed eyes, deep breaths, and a *namaste*.

I waited for our next test stress experience to introduce what I referred to as a "Zen moment." We all closed our eyes and raised our arms toward the heavens, bending them at the elbow with index finger and thumb touching. A few deep breaths and an "Om" sound and we all felt much better and ready to take on the task at hand. This was great, but I wanted to take it further. I wanted something that would keep the calmness going throughout the duration of the test.

I came up with the Gregorian chant. It wasn't a kind of music that everyone had heard (let alone heard of at all). For anyone in the above category: the Gregorian chant is Christian music going back to the sixth century, used at Mass to celebrate various religious occasions. I assume it was started by a pope named Gregory. For me, it was second only to yoga in ability to give stress relief. I remember sitting in church with my list of daydreams, squirming on the hard, wooden pew. The Mass was in Latin then, and the priest's back was all I could see—that is, if I could see over the back of the person sitting in front of me. Why do people with dandruff wear black? Do they have any idea how distracting that is when it's all someone else has to look at? Anyway, I remembered when the Gregorian chants started I would slowly find a sense of peace, a feeling of calm. I'd stop the daydreams. I'd stop counting the little white specks that decorated the jacket from shoulder to shoulder of the soul seated ahead of me. It was perfect. It was composure. It was the universal "Om" extended and put to music. Its simple melody, its repetition of a small gamut of notes sung in a language I couldn't understand brought on the feeling. It was worth a try.

Of course, there was the division of church and state issue to consider. This was just at the time when prayer was beginning to go the way of the dodo and Christmas carols and the utterance of the word "God" were under heavy surveillance in schools. We were already dabbling with Eastern Zen and now I was really pushing the envelope. I decided the best road to peace and tranquility on all fronts was to skip over the chant's religious connotation. I explained to the students that this music, when played in the background, could possibly help them focus and be more relaxed when taking a test. I kept the description fairly vague, not wanting to wade into murky religious waters. I was careful with my words and the inflection in my voice and delicately skipped over the original purpose of the music. I wasn't surprised when I played the students a chant, they hated it. I told them they didn't have to like it; they just had to see if it helped them when they were being tested.

They humored me as always and tried out the music on their first few tests. There were no further comments about it until one day when we were doing silent reading. On their own, the students preceded opening their books with a "Zen moment" and then asked if I would put on that Halloween music while they read.

"What Halloween music?" I asked.

"The Halloween music you play when we take a test. It does help like you said."

I didn't know if I should laugh, make a quick sign of the cross, or say a silent *namaste*.

"Halloween music" was a perfect name for the chants, so Halloween music it became. For the kids, the chants didn't remove the stress, it helped them conquer it. It reminded them of the holiday when you could giggle in the face of fear, laugh at your worst nightmare— when the horrific is greeted with pleasantries and treats. I ignored the fact of its origins as a pagan holiday that was later adopted by the Christians. I took a leap of faith and decided that some things just had to be overlooked for the greater good. After all, why make so much ado about nothing? Isn't that really what causes so much of our stress?

First Day Teaching in the Closet
(not what you think)

There are the student comments college never prepares you for—the ones where you have to use life-skills, from-your-gut, wing-it responses. There's a big chance you won't pick the best answer, but coming up with one that even remotely fits should be worth some points…at least one that leaves the child feeling like he or she got something out of it.

My first one of these came on my first day teaching. I taught at a grammar school in the morning and a middle school in the afternoon. At the middle school, my room was a vacant closet with "Storage" written across the door. I wanted to place a "Miss" in front of it, but being new, I wasn't sure what the humor range was of my fellow academics.

I set up my desk as best I could and waited for my first student to arrive. My caseload list and Individual Educational Program (IEP, an official legal document) stated that she was a seventh-grade girl who needed assistance in math. She arrived on time, took a seat on the other side of my desk—the only desk in the room—and stated, "Hi, I'm June. Do you fuck?"

Okay…I wanted to say, "Hi, I'm Miss Storage, and I'm out of here right now." But instead, I silently searched for a plan B—which turned out to be telling her my name and responding to her question with "that's none of your business."

This didn't seem to daunt her. She kept right on going with a smile and a comment of "I do."

This was an obvious case of too much information. I answered, "That's none of *my* business. We're here to do math." I smiled and opened the math book. She got right to work. I'm sure there was an array of more appropriate responses, but like I said, it was my first day and I was never taught this in college. Bottom line? She was doing math. I counted that as mission accomplished.

Do You See What I See

Grammar school kids are always so amazed when they see you outside of school. I remember feeling amazed at that too when I was their age. It's the moment when kids realize teachers don't live at school and actually do stuff ordinary people do, like go to the movies, go food shopping, drive like idiots, walk their dogs.

I ran into one of my students outside a doughnut shop one Saturday. He froze—but probably not because I had a cup of coffee in my hand. I *always* had a cup of coffee in my hand. I think it was the car keys in the other hand that appeared foreign and the fact that I could live and breathe in the world outside of school. I smiled and gave him a big hello, but he just stared and remained speechless.

The next Monday, I spotted him in the hallway. He called out to me, all excited. "Miss Iaccarino, Miss Iaccarino, you'll never guess who I saw in front of the doughnut shop this Saturday." If he hadn't been so genuinely excited, I would have taken this as a trick question.

"Who?" I asked with a bit of trepidation.

He looked at me as if giving me some incredible piece of information and said, "Miss Iaccarino!" Apart from having a bit of a split-identity crisis, I panicked, because judging by the expression on his face, he was waiting for a reply.

"Wow," I said, "I saw her there too." He was pleased that we both saw me that Saturday morning and he left a contented little boy. I just wasn't sure how *I* felt.

Very Interesting

Sometimes, no matter how wrong a child's answer was, I just couldn't get myself to be negative about it. I'd try to find some way to use that answer to help guide the student to the right one.

On one particular day, I just went with total avoidance. It was a math group. The topic was "greater than, smaller than." I wrote the numerals "8" and "80" on the board. I like to start with something that is obvious. I said, "Now, which one is bigger or greater: eight or eighty?" I used my arms for effect, pulling my hands close together for "eight" and stretching out my arms for "eighty." I even said "eighty" *louder* than "eight." I figured I had covered it all for the visual, kinesthetic, and auditory learner.

Most of the kids were looking at me with a blank stare. I wasn't sure if they were thinking, *Is she kidding or what?* Or maybe they were just bored senseless. I didn't give up and repeated the question three more times, exactly the same way. All of a sudden, one girl's hand went popping up straight as an arrow with her arm stretching toward the heavens. "Ooh, ooh," she kept saying, with that *Look at me! Look at me!* expression on her face.

I smiled, called on her, and said, "Okay, which one is greater? Eight or eighty?"

She stood up proud as punch and called out, "Yes!"

The answer took my breath away. "Wow," I finally managed to say. "That is a really interesting answer. Very interesting. Okay, let's put your papers away and play our favorite card game, Addition War."

Sometimes avoidance is your only option.

Clogged Vowels

There was a second grader in one of my groups who, like so many others in reading, was having a horrific time associating the letters with the sounds they made, especially the vowels. He was a trouper, though, always trying and always staying optimistic.

He was out for a few weeks. I was told he had been admitted to the hospital. I was so happy to see him when he came back. He was all smiles and told me he had surgery that was going to help him read. All I could think of was brain surgery, but I was completely at the wrong end of the operating table. He had, I quote: "Clogged vowels." To which he added, "That's why I couldn't read!"

If only it were that easy!

Two for the Price of One

I taught next door to another special-ed resource teacher for many years. We made a great team and I loved working with her. Her Polish last name, ending in the common "-ski," was about as difficult as my own Italian last name with all the vowels—until one student we both knew came up with his own solution and his own pronunciation. Whenever he saw either one of us, he would say "Hi, Ms. Iaccaluski." We'd smile, say hello, and leave it at that. After all, we'd been called a lot worse.

.....

All teachers know, as does everyone else, there's a good answer, an appropriate answer, the best answer...and sometimes an "I just couldn't resist" answer. That's the answer that you know you probably shouldn't say, but given the opportunity, you just can't stop yourself.

Nathan Hale and Match.com

I had a fifth-grade student once who I was helping study for a social studies test. It was on the Revolutionary War. We were on the famous people part, focusing on Nathan Hale. Wanting her to connect with Nathan Hale, I went on and on about his background. I told her how he was a teacher and how he lived right here in Connecticut and even went to Yale University. I explained how there was a fantastic statue of him right on the Yale campus and Nathan was actually quite a good-looking man.

She looked at me intently the entire time I was speaking. She was completely focused on everything I was saying and I knew she was totally into it. When I finished, I asked her if she had any questions. I was pretty sure I had covered everything, every detail clearly and to perfection, so I was surprised when she said yes, in fact she did have a question.

And so she asked, "Did you know him?"

I couldn't believe it! Did I look over two hundred years old? The worst part was that she wasn't joking. She was dead serious. Me, sitting around one of the staff room tables with old Nate, quill, and parchment, writing up IEPs together. I looked at her just as seriously and out of nowhere came an answer that just poured forth.

"No," I said, "I didn't know him. But my grandmother dated him a few times." I'm not sure where that came from, but I just couldn't resist.

Fun with Dick and Jane

Then there are those times when you say something to the class you don't even realize you're saying. What is that called? Oh yes, a "double entendre." Which turns into a huge faux pas.

.....

Along with being completely floored at what kids say, there are those times when we can't believe what is coming out of our own mouths. During my research room teacher days, I thought it would be nice to show the kids the books I read when *I* was in second grade. I actually found some of the Dick and Jane series buried in the back of a storage closet. I was also curious to see how they felt about the stories. So, one day, I stood at the head of the table where my second-grade students were sitting and presented the book. My guardian-angel paraprofessional sat across from me. She was also interested to see what the kids thought.

I held up the book and gave them some nostalgic history about the background of the book and its characters. We looked at some of the drawings to see if the second graders noticed any differences between the clothes and household items and such and what they had in the present. We talked about how pictures give a visual clue to what a story is about. I randomly opened to a picture of Dick standing behind his father. This was my first mistake.

The picture showed Dick hiding behind his father while they stood outside looking at a tree. Their backs were to the viewers. Propped up against the tree was Dick's football uniform and helmet, both filled with paper. The point of the picture was to show Dick playing a joke on his father, trying to make him believe that he was sleeping by the tree instead of standing right behind him. This could be pretty funny to kids, especially since the father was calling out to the football uniform, telling it to wake up.

I announced to the kids, "Look! His dad is talking to a stuffed Dick!" I paused. Did I really say that? I surveyed my second graders. Judging by the looks on their faces, the comment appeared to have gone over their heads. My Para, however, was rubbing her neck, something she did when she was nervous. Her eyes were huge and she was staring at me. I told the kids I had to leave for a moment and motioned for her to come with me.

I closed the door once we were outside and she blurted out, "Stuffed Dick!" I can't believe you said "Stuffed Dick." We cracked up in giddy, nervous laughter, then composed ourselves and went back into the room.

I quickly turned to another page. The image looked innocent enough. It showed a three-legged race with Sally and Jane hopping along in a cloth sack. None of the kids had ever been in a three-legged race, so I explained to them, "It really is fun to hop in the sack with someone." At this point my Para stood up, took the book out of my hand, and said that we had had enough fun with Dick and Jane for the day. The books went back into the storage closet.

.....

I know teachers, especially teachers of younger grades, have the reputation of talking to people like they are all second graders. You know, like the old joke about how young mothers cut their husbands' meat when they're out to dinner. So this is in defense of all teachers who have been shunned, ridiculed, snickered at, and eye rolled through the years for slowly and carefully pointing out every minuscule detail ad nauseam when speaking to their peers. They know you never, ever assume or take for granted that people get the point of what you are saying.

Out of the Mouths of Babes

One example—and I will try to keep it simple—was from a third grader.

I told my small group of students that I was going to pass out a ditto to them. I then asked if they knew what a ditto was. That was the "don't assume anything" question. One student's hand shot up and he replied, "A ditto is what a teacher gives you when she can't think of anything else to do." All right, perhaps there was a small bit of truth in his statement. Needless to say, I skipped doing the ditto.

Here's another assumption: that *you* know what a ditto is. Nobody uses that word anymore. Now they're called "copies." This makes perfect sense, since ditto machines have been replaced by copy machines and printers, just like the way records were replaced with tapes and tapes were replaced with CDs and they were replaced with ipods. The music pretty much sounds the same; it's just the way we get to listen to it has changed.

Still, there is one way copies are pretty much like dittos, so I try not to use them either.

Water

Another time, I picked up on my caseload a third-grade girl. She was incredibly interesting. Her visual memory was pretty good, but she showed some deficits in the auditory areas. The problem manifested itself with sound-symbol association (I'm trying not to use small words and be insulting). If she didn't know the word visually, she would read it as a different word making absolutely no connection with the sounds of the letters she was looking at. Still following? Okay. For example, if the word was "problem" and she didn't know it visually, she would say "count" or whatever came to mind or might fit the content area.

I exhausted a large amount of different approaches. I ended up using my old favorite, finger spelling, a technique used for speaking to the deaf. It was a bit of a slow start, but it was all I had left, so I kept going. Then, out of the blue one day while finger spelling various words, she blurted out, "I get it!" *Please! Let this be true!* She looked up at me and started to explain. "Every letter makes a certain sound and those are the sounds that make up the word."

I had an inkling of how Annie Sullivan felt as Helen Keller finger-spelled "water." She got it! What amazed me was how she had missed it in the first place. Where along the line did we forget to tell her the first rule of reading? And even if we had told her, why didn't we notice that she didn't understand it?

Forget all this testing. Every teacher should be supplied with a simple, "common sense" checklist to give to each child. Then we can give it to our peers and the woman at dinner who's cutting her husband's meat. You can never be too sure.

Teaching Abroad

(not to be confused with teaching a broad)

In the fall of 2000 I had the wonderful opportunity to teach at a university in China for a week as a guest lecturer on American culture. After my school system's approval, I packed my bags and all the necessary volumes of paperwork, met up with three others (one of whom was a very dear friend), and headed out on Thanksgiving Day. It was an amazing trip —so amazing, it was worth the exhaustion I had for a few weeks afterward.

I arrived with a suitcase full of candy to use for tips and gifts, my academic material, clothes, and the four words of Chinese I had managed to learn. I was the first of us to walk through customs, so once past it, I stopped to wait for the group. I heard a man yelling behind me, so I turned to look. There stood a Chinese soldier with a rifle pointed in my direction. Unfortunately, none of the words he was yelling were any of the four I knew, so I dropped my bags and raised my hands in the air. This was not exactly the welcome I had expected. I used my index finger to point to myself, saying, "Me? You want me?" I have no idea what he yelled back, so I kept my hands high in the air.

Coming right behind my captor was my very dear friend, who was laughing hysterically. As I was considering reviewing my choice of friends, I realized that the soldier was cracking a smile. I turned my head around and noticed that there was a man behind me who also had his hands up in the air. I took an educated guess that I was not the one under arrest and tried to make a quiet exit. This wasn't too easy after making the biggest faux pas in China: embarrassing oneself. But I tried to look at the bright side: the worst was over. Other than tripping and falling at "The Mouth of the Dragon" (also known as the beginning of the Great Wall, ergo the joke about my "great fall at the Great Wall") and making the mistake of using the word "sex" instead of "yes" (obviously not a word I learned correctly) at a dinner in our honor on the last night, everything went well and the rest of the trip was devoid of any more embarrassing moments.

There were adjustments to be made for not only the language barriers but the style barriers of everyday living. We all tried to just go with the flow. Let's just say that when I got home and showed my family photos of the trip, my brother asked why I had taken a picture of a car wash. I looked at it and explained, "That's not a car wash, that's my hotel." I smiled at the thought of the "car wash" and the priceless memories that went with it.

I loved the students and could only hope they were learning as much from me as I was from them. They all knew English and were more than willing to speak it once I said my four words of Chinese. They were assured that I would never laugh at their English, even when they pronounced my first name "Catife." I took tons of photos, and every chance I had, I purchased items that I could bring back to show my fifth-grade students when I returned.

Once home, I created a unit on my trip to share with the kids. We spent part of each session talking about it, using the globe, Chinese characters (which are used for writing words), visual aids, and little stories. We went over the Chinese New Year, different aspects of the culture, and landmarks. I told them how the college students learned the Hokey Pokey. On the last day, I brought in photos I had taken of my students there. They all leaned close for a good look.

All of a sudden, Alice let out a cry of "Oh my God!"

Was there something obscene that I had missed in the photo? Was there someone giving the Chinese finger that I didn't know about? "What?" I asked, looking at her, sure by her wide eyes staring at the photo that she saw something shocking.

My shock was just short of her own when she answered, "Look! They're all Chinese!"

"Ya think?" was what I wanted to say. *Duh!*

With all the work I did for that unit, had I forgotten to state the obvious? Maybe not, I thought later. Maybe it wasn't stating the obvious that I was missing; maybe it was seeing the obvious. Alice was actually making a wonderful observational statement and compliment to American culture. For her, being American had nothing to do with race, religion, or heritage. Alice was so completely engrossed in her culture that she had no reason to assume that other countries were different from ours. Maybe Alice should have gone to China to teach my course. I learned a lot from her about our culture that day.

.....

My four words of Chinese—or more specifically, phrases—were, "Hello," "Thank you," "How much," and "I don't understand." Good words to know.

When all was said and done about what was said and done, I came to the conclusion that...

2

Honesty Was the Best Policy

Along with catchy phrases, there are many little pithy truisms and idiomatic expressions that travel with us through life like bad pennies…some of which end up in the laps of both teachers and parents. They pop up at us, and though we feel like we need them like a hole in the head, we must take heed. That is, of course, excluding "Spare the rod, spoil the child." I wouldn't touch that one with a ten-foot pole. Not sparing the rod comes under the category of abuse. Times do change.

However, "Children should be seen and not heard" is one that many of us often wish were put into law. Just ask any lunchroom teacher or school bus driver, and they'll tell you it should come right after the First Amendment. Two other phrases that have managed to withstand time among teachers are "You're not there to be their friend," and "They don't have to like you, but they should respect you." I don't know if there's a standard way to put these, which I guess shows how much I really paid attention to them.

I doubt, though, anyone can forget the old favorite "Honesty is the best policy." It travels with us our whole lives. I do have to mention here, though, that I once received a thank-you card from a group I had spent my lunchtime teaching to knit. It stated that I was their favorite and best teacher. I was so touched. Before reading further, I started to mentally review my dream list of what could qualify me for this esteemed category. What they wrote, however, was not on the list. It caught me completely by surprise. There, a caring hand had meticulously written the words, "You never lie." I was as stunned as I was touched. Are teachers perceived like commercials? Things that go on and on, trying to sell something or pitch information that isn't necessarily true?

Let's face it, though, honesty can be tricky and subject to some gray areas, especially with kids. Some honest facts they may not be ready to hear, so a bit of a fib or truth stretching is mandatory until they are old enough to hear that specific truth. After all, Rome was not built in a day. When a third-grade student asked what "intercourse" was, I explained that it was a way of communicating—like talking—and then bored the child to death with my lengthy speech on the subject of verbal intercourse. When a first-grade boy asked what "sex" was, I answered, "It's a label for 'boy' or 'girl'," and explained that he would see the word *sex* on future job applications and should check off "male."

These are the gray areas of intercourse and sex…or just some boys and girls communicating.

I Don't Like You

I considered times in my teaching career when telling the truth had actually worked out for the best, even when lying would have been a better choice. One occasion comes to mind first: I had a small group of third-grade students. One boy had being pleasantly obstinate down to an art form. He just politely refused to do anything. I kept him after one day and asked him why he refused to do his work. He gave me a five-word answer: "Because I don't like you." Well, that's an honest answer, and I decided I owed him nothing less. So I gave him a seven-word honest answer.

"That's okay, because I don't like you either." It should be noted that we both spoke with a tone devoid of any animosity, like we were discussing the weather.

He looked surprised though, possibly at my honesty. He said, "You don't?"

"No, I don't," I answered, and added, "and that's okay. You don't have to like everyone. Some people just don't like each other for no reason at all, like you and me. There's nothing wrong with that; it's just the way we feel." He listened politely and took this piece of information to heart.

Returning to the "respect" truism, I then added that the fact was, we were going to have to work together the rest of the year, and we were going to have to respect that fact and respect each other in the process. He could respect me for trying my best to teach him, and I could respect him for trying his best to learn. So, there and then, we shook hands and sealed a deal to continue to not like each other but respect each other.

The rest of the year went great. At the end he came up to me, shook my hand, and said that he still didn't like me. I shook his hand back and said that was okay, I still didn't like him, but it was a pleasure working with him. He smiled and agreed. There it was: all three truisms put into effect. We didn't like each other. We did respect each other. And we were very honest about it.

I guess they are called truisms for a reason, or at least it seemed so on this occasion. I can pretty much vouch, though, that honesty doesn't work all the time, but it shouldn't be completely ignored. There is a time and place for everything, even honesty. Scout's honor.

Charm School

During my first ten years of teaching, I developed an after-school program called "Charm School." That, of course, would never work now. It is so antiquated. Life at present revolves around reality shows, and as popular as they are, there is nothing charming about them. Rude, loud, inarticulate, and obnoxious are all in vogue now; just watch some news channels and some politicians. To be perfectly honest, I was surprised at how many students, even way, way back then, who were not only interested in Charm School, but enjoyed it! Maybe it was just a novelty to them, something foreign they could learn about.

It started small: just sitting around a table with some fifth-grade girls talking about the proper way to do things like eating and sitting and how to use words such as "please" and "thank you." One day I was telling them that when you are at the table and you need something (for instance, the bread), it is proper to say, "Would you please pass the bread?"

One girl looked very pensive at this news and said, "You know, I always thought that's what you're supposed to say. So, the other night I asked my dad to please pass the salt and he told me to get off my fuckin' ass and get it myself." I seriously thought of expanding Charm School to include some parents.

By my last year of Charm School I did expand it—not to parents but to boys. This was done at their own request, which was an unexpected surprise for me. I made a mental note to be less sexist in the future. We had guest speakers from a gym, skin care spa, and a modeling school. There was a fashion show at the end for which a store lent us clothes, and the kids made the newspaper. Teachers also joined in to teach the classes. The more the students got into it, the more instruction we included, even covering things like the proper way to answer a phone—"Yo," "Yeah," and "What?" being replaced with a cheerful "Hello." We went to restaurants and borrowed menus that were written on paper and not on walls, and we served potatoes that were eaten with a fork instead of fingers. The kids were completely intrigued and we were so proud of them.

We even extended to a higher level past outward charm to inner beauty and included a class on self-esteem. Each teacher took a group of about seven students; we all had to write five things that we liked and disliked about ourselves. Then we read them out loud and discussed them. There were no sarcastic giggles or smirks because no one was exempt from sharing, not even the staff. Having to put yourself in the position of self-inflicted scrutiny breeds a kinder view of others' idiosyncrasies, and everyone treaded more gently so as not to step on someone else's faults.

One girl wrote the thing she liked least about herself was nobody liked her because she was ugly. She was right about nobody liking her. She had a tendency to be rather sour, rude, pushy, and mean-spirited, but she was absolutely beautiful. Like everyone else's at the table, my mouth dropped. "How can you say you're ugly? You are one of the prettiest girls in this school." The other girls confirmed this with headshakes or verbal praise of her outstanding features.

"So how come nobody likes me?" she asked, completely baffled.

"Nobody likes you because you have a tendency to be rude and obnoxious," I answered nicely and without any undertone of meanness. The rest of the girls shook their heads in agreement, also void of any meanness. We all waited a moment and held our breaths to see how she was going to take the news.

She sat up straight in her chair and smiled. "You mean, I'm not ugly?"

"You're a vision of beauty," I told her. All the girls started saying how they loved her hair, her eyes. They even went as far as to say they were a little jealous and wanted to be as pretty as she was. We charmed her with honesty. We then told her everything she did that was rude and annoying. This is where she learned "It's not what you say, it's how you say it." We formed a pact that every time she did something rude we'd give a secret signal so she would know to stop. She loved the idea.

Something wonderful happened that day. She made friends. These girls took her under their wings. They were going to help her succeed. With her success came their success. She was happy for the first time all year. If beauty is in the eyes of the beholder, then this was the first time she beheld her own beauty. She kept that stunning presence inside and out, sharing it with others, including me—even into adulthood.

Maybe manners and little acts of honest kindness are not in style or in the curriculum, but maybe they should be. They do dull the edge of anger. There is power in pleasantness. A please, a thank you, a compliment, a hello, all have the power to make someone smile and feel acknowledged. It's the power of politeness, and it can work like a charm.

Trust

Along with a little honesty and respect, there is the trust factor. Other than the one about God, I'm sure there's a truism about trust out there somewhere, I just can't think of one at the moment. Nevertheless, the trust factor can be very powerful—or so I learned from a second grader. She was doing much better in spelling, and I was considerably pleased about this. She went from D's to A's on the tests. Boy, did I think I was just the teacher of the year. After every test I would fill her ears with words of praise. That is, until one of the other kids ratted on her and said she had a list of the words on her lap while taking the test. I was livid. I read her the riot act.

I look back and think that perhaps just a touch of my anger was as much ego as disappointment. I carried on about how cheating was like lying and that when you lie you are not being honest and that when you are not honest you lose someone's trust and losing someone's trust was the worst thing you could ever lose. I guess my rather verbose sentence went a bit over the top, because she was in tears with her head resting on the desk. The other kids commented in sympathy for her tears. I said that losing someone's trust was something worth crying about.

The next week, she traveled in and out of my class with hand on heart, pledging to show me that she would earn back my trust. She came in on Friday saying she was going to make me proud and beamed through the entire spelling test. Holding the paper like an olive branch and anticipation on her face, she handed it to me to be corrected. I corrected it, shocked and disappointed at how many she got wrong. Her final grade was a very low D. I couldn't figure out if this was some type of joke or not. I told her she had a D and she kept smiling. I was missing something here, I was sure of it. I asked her why she was smiling. She said, "I got a D. That shows you I didn't cheat. Do I have your trust back?" I had to return a smile and said yes, she had my trust back. I watched her return to her seat, so proud, so happy.

The long and the short of it was that my trust meant more to her than a good grade. She had taken to heart what I had said about trust being so important, so much so that she placed achieving trust over achieving a good grade. She learned an important lesson, and so did I. I had only half done my job: somehow I hadn't quite gotten across the point that it was cheating we wanted to change, not the better grade. I guess that just got lost in translation.

3

Literally Speaking

The students I found the most fascinating were the "literal translators." They can really give you pause and make you think of how you use everyday words and turns of phrase. They can also be incredibly frustrating and annoying to most teachers and parents, but just think about what it's like for *them*. They might think of a "cowboy" as some type of grotesque with the body of a cow and the upper torso of a boy. "Do you want to play cowboys?" could be a frightening question. The "mailman" just sounds redundant, and the term "face off'" could cause an unnecessary fear of some sports. So many of our common signs could be taken to mean something completely different. Think about it and take another look at "drive-through window," "Slow Children," "Slow: Men at Work." And what about "park on the driveway" and "drive on the parkway"? Then there's always my favorite that has popped up in schools since peanut allergies have become so severe: "No nuts in this room."

The Wind Doesn't Run

I was working with James, a sweet boy if a bit overly methodical. You couldn't help but like him, and with all his little idiosyncrasies, the other kids liked him too. He showed up to my resource room without his favorite pencil. He couldn't work without it. I mean, he *really* couldn't work without it. All he could focus on was the pencil. I tried to entice him with a new one, but that wasn't working. I finally relented and said "Okay, James, you can go back and get it this time. Don't let it happen again. Go ahead, but run like the wind."

He looked at me like I had just told him to jump off a bridge. "No! No!" he yelled, pounding his fists on the desk. "No! No!" he repeated.

"No, what?" I asked.

He responded with the most obvious of truths: "Wind doesn't run, water runs." Duh! I should have known that.

"Okay, James. Run like the water." I smiled. He smiled back and off he went.

For the rest of the year, everyone ran like the water. After all, the wind doesn't run, it blows. Water runs. I realize that now. Good thing I didn't tell him his nose was running!

.....

If You Can't Beat Them, Join Them

Literally speaking students, however, can be a great tool for learning how to teach. After all, they are telling you exactly *what they hear and how they process your words. I tried it and, as strange as it seems, it worked. It not only worked on literal students, it worked on the rest. Literally speaking: "Live and learn."*

In Your Head

Many years before James, there was Kevin. He was a second-grade student struggling with reading and spelling. I was struggling with finding a way to teach him reading and spelling. Nothing in my little bag of academic tricks was working. Out of desperation, I opted for the old standby: constantly repeating spelling words and having him write them, yes, five times each. After we were both bored to death, I tried giving him the practice test one more time. He didn't pass. It felt like a slow and painful death, and we were both way too young for that to happen.

I even tried the accentuated pronunciation technique. That's where I say the word very slowly, stopping at the end of each syllable, even saying the silent letters. I sounded like some old record played at the wrong speed. "Listen" became "liss-ten." Along with slow, I added loud for effect, the way some do when talking to a non-English speaker. I wrote the word in syllables on a piece of paper, underlining "is" and "ten" as "little words" within the word. After that, I made a story out of it. "Bob is five. *L is ten.*"

It was hopeless. He spelled it wrong yet again. I smiled (with gritted teeth) and spelled the word *listen* for him one more time. In frustration, he dropped his pencil, looked at me, and said "But how do you know that?"

Now *I* was confused. "Know what?" I asked.

"How do you know how to spell it?" he clarified, looking at me with big eyes, as if I carried some great, magical secret.

"It's in my head," I answered. I have to admit that I was a bit stumped by the question and had to ponder a second just how I did know that. It was this oversimplified response that worked the charm.

The next thing I knew, he had his eyeball pressed up against my ear. I calmly asked him why he was doing that. He answered, "But I don't see it."

"See what?" I asked, sitting perfectly still and hoping no one walked by, only to write me up for some inappropriate act like having a student look into my ear. I'm sure there must be some lawsuit waiting to happen with that one.

His next words came across loud and clear, due to their proximity to my ear. "I don't see the word 'listen' in your head." That was it! The answer I was looking for. First, I gently removed him from myself and had him sit down. I leaned toward him and gave my most serious look. I told him that even though he couldn't see it, the word was there. I told him the word was in his head, too—he just had to go find it. I told him to close his eyes and go look in his head for the word "listen."

Being the great kid that he was, he indulged my request and closed his eyes. He leaned back his head for some extra help. Next thing he said was, "Listen. L-i-s-t-e-n, listen."

From then on, whenever Kevin said he didn't know the answer to something we studied in reading and spelling, I would simply say, "Yes you do, it's in your head. Go look." Look he did, and somewhere in his head he found the answer. He was so proud, so happy that he now knew how to retrieve information. All he had to do was look in his head. Why didn't I ever think of that before? It's so obvious!

I decided to take this idea and run with it...like the water, of course. It was my new teaching strategy. A little tweaking here and there, an addition of a few filing cabinets, folders, and sometimes a room labeled "In My Head" were added for dramatic effect and just for fun. When all else failed, I went to the masters of imagination, the students themselves. Once they got the hang of it, it was no holds barred.

Those Odd Moments

Karen was the queen of "in-your-head" sorting skills. Stacy, her classmate in math, was stumped on how to remember what odd and even numbers were. I was completely out of clues, so I asked Karen how she did it. Pleased as punch to be asked, she looked at Stacy and, speaking with her adorable lisp and speech impediment, she explained how she kept "all the odd numbers on the wight side of my head and all the even numbers on the weft side of my head." The best part was when she wanted to know the odd numbers: she would pull on her left ear. And when she wanted to know the even numbers, she pulled on her right ear. *You've got to be kidding*! was all I could think. Stacy, on the other hand, was grinning from weft ear to wight and spent the next few days pulling those ears and reciting the numbers until the day of the test.

On that day, I watched her become very nervous. She raised her hand and ever so seriously said, "I know one, three, five, seven, nine is one and two, four, six, eight, ten is the other, but I can't remember which one is odd." She swallowed hard. "Do you think it would be cheating if I asked Karen to pull her odd ear?" I was willing to bet it was the first time a teacher had ever been asked that question. Judging by the smile of pride on Karen's face, I figured she didn't take the "*odd* ear" comment as an insult. I smiled and shook my head yes. Karen pulled her ear; Stacy smiled and wrote down the correct answer. I definitely looked at this as not cheating. It was in Stacy's head all the time; she just needed a little help finding it. Okay, so maybe it was cheating, but it was just a little.

.....

Sometimes it's not what is said, but what isn't—*that inspires you to change the course of the lesson and literally do what you think is best.*

Boring

In the classroom, it is difficult to compete with everything else in the outside world, including what students bring to school. They have a tireless fund of immediate gratification afforded them with bells and whistles on their computers, iTunes, cell phones, the Wii, ipad, and all the rest that I can't think of or just am not savvy to.

They sit there and look at us, not able to change the channel, put us on rewind, fast forward, mute, pause, or completely turn us off. So they just tune us out. We are there—one person, few props, and what we are given to present to them—and many times it all seems to them as interesting or useful as a commercial for mortgage insurance. Mind you, school was never under any obligation to be exciting or entertaining, and compared to previous generations of students, this one has it pretty good. Previous generations of teachers, however, never had to compete with what this one has to. So we get to be even more boring than ever.

Some of us try very hard to stimulate some excitement and interest. Years ago, when teaching some first graders to be "clock wise" I had them all stand before the clock. One hand on hip, one raised in the air in a true disco pose, we moved our hips and our arms waved from number to number, singing in chorus as we rocked around the clock. There were many other methods, some original, some I borrowed from others. I was not alone. We hunted everywhere for something to raise enthusiasm. Really, this is true. We've even gone so far as to work our wardrobes around curriculum;

the more lackluster the material, the more lavish our fabrics. I was known for donning some pretty creative ensembles.

Luckily for me, most of my students knew I really was trying to conquer the doldrums and were pretty patient when it came to the tedious. If one stated, "This is boring," I would usually answer, "You're bored? Well, I already know this stuff, so think how bored *I* am." I'd throw in some hair pulling and face scrunching for effect and then add, "So the sooner you learn it the less bored we will all be." Perhaps it was just the confirmation that yes indeed, it was boring, that put them at ease. Or maybe they were nervous I'd be bald by the end of the year. Either way, they got back to work.

In all fairness to students who are learning in this age after Aquarius, there *is* some pretty wearisome curriculum out there. Even my Tibetan top, bolero pants, and high top sneakers could not manage to light a spark of interest. I even have to say there were times when I was so amazed that the students not only didn't revolt, they actually kept plying through the gray, dismal waters of tedium. So focused on learning was one group I even had to take the boring bull by the horns and provoke a rebellion.

This group and I were forced by curriculum guidelines to partake in a new reading series. Let me say right now, I am not protesting against reading series. There are some great ones out there; teachers know which they are. Believe me, this was not one of them. I followed my usual routine for reading. I made a copy of a page from the story so that no one was tempted to mark up a book. The kids could silent read first, highlighting the words they didn't know so we could use those for our vocabulary, reading, and spelling list. They didn't mind this so much because I had told them the more words they highlighted, the more words they would learn, and it was a really good thing. We would then do speed drills with the words, divide them into syllables when needed, and write the word phonetically for those ad-nauseam exceptions to the rules. Once they had all the clues written on their papers and could read the passage comfortably, we read it one more time from the book. All that being said, On this particular day, we were reading out loud from our copies for the final time.

The third student was taking a turn. My eyes were closing and I held my copy close to my face to hide my yawn. The only thing that kept me awake and not wishing I was at the dentist office having a root canal was the bewildering fact that the kids were still doing their utmost not to be completely sedated by this painfully inane story. I couldn't put them, or me, through this a moment longer. I politely interrupted the reader and asked, "You know what I think of this story?" The kids seemed to emerge a bit from their trancelike state and looked at me quizzically. I took that as a no, they didn't know what I thought. So I continued, "I think this story is *boring*!" and I threw the papers over my head and onto the floor. I'm not sure the readers were stunned or still under the daze of dreariness, but they didn't quite give me the reaction I expected. "So," I asked, with a bit of *I dare you* in my voice and a coy smile, "What do *you* think of this story?"

They all read my mind, if not my face, and together as one they called out with complete, renewed, pure joy: "*Boring!*" and flung the papers over their heads onto the floor.

We were now on a mission. We collaborated as a team. I placed three or four different types of books on the table and we perused each one. Our choice was an old, stand-the-test-of-time classic chapter book. It was by far a more difficult read than what we had had before. They loved it. New words were filling the blackboard, voices were laced with expression and purpose inhaled from each page, and I got to go out and buy a whole new wardrobe in every shade of gray and black. I could now be a classic dresser, and they could be excited and successful in the subject of reading. It was a win-win.

It was also a huge learning experience. Boring is all relative. If I had started out with our chapter book choice, they would probably have more than liked it eventually, but chances are they would have resisted it too at first. So start them out with something easier but incredibly dull, then take that away and give them a choice and an interesting challenge. In their world, they had control of the remote. Together we pressed *Pause*, *Erase*, and *Menu* and picked something new to play. I guess that mandated reading series had a purpose after all. By not using it, the kids learned so much. Maybe that's why it was mandated. Maybe it should have come with a remote. Just a thought.

The Hole Number

Maybe we should listen a little closer to the literal thinker and then stretch the concept out to the entire class. We know what we say to them makes sense, but do we know if what we say is actually what they perceive? Take that very common mathematical term, the "whole number." We teach children to add and subtract from the "whole number." There is one math program that even refers to it as just "the whole." So, the first question to students looking at an addition or subtraction example is "What's the whole?"

Now, let's think like a child and look at it from a kindergarten-to-maybe-second-grader's point of view, and what he or she might actually perceive. Children's most common knowledge associated with the sound of the word "whole" is of something you dig or have in your sock, or something to do with a doughnut. So, the "whole" number becomes the "hole" number. It's a number with something missing, the exact opposite of what we call an "entire" number. Maybe we should call it the "full" number.

We could fill a measuring cup with water up to the one-cup mark. We could then ask the class, "How full of water is the cup?" After the kids give us an answer, we inform them that the cup is like the "full" number. Then we could pour some out for subtraction or put some in for addition. Then maybe we could run like the water with all those "hole" number problems.

PART II
Behavior in the Manner of Speaking

*

Separation anxiety

4

Punish the Behavior, Not the Child

Almost Sounds Like Exorcism

Buzz phrases are easy to remember but sometimes a bit confusing to understand. One that sticks out the most is "Punish the behavior, not the child." It causes more than a few moments of serious pondering. I mean, I'm a teacher, not an exorcist. I thought of that clever question always asked in Philosophy 101: "If a tree falls in the woods and there is no one there to hear it, does it make a sound?" Can I even separate that tree from the forest or the forest from the tree? The mediaeval whipping boy came to mind too. A prince could not be punished due to his royal status, so they had what's called a "whipping boy." He got hit instead of the prince, sort of a beating by proxy. I didn't know if "punishing the behavior, not the child" worked for the child, but it was causing me some severe pangs of separation stress. I knew one thing for sure: I was immediately ruling out exorcism. I saw the movie. I wasn't going there.

When all else is said and done, "punish the behavior, not the child" does make sense. It's a mind-set, a choice of words and even voice. It leaves you open to discourage a child from planning some payback while sitting in time-out. A lot has to do with the language you use.

I Need to Help You

I had a third grader in a small reading group who thought his time with me was a social hour. My "punish the behavior, not the child" choice of words went something like this: "I need to find a way to help you focus. Let's try having you sit at the other table by yourself and see if that works. I hope it does, because I really want you to do well." Then I added for support, "Most of all, Friday is free-time day, and I would hate for you to be left out." He got up and went to the other table. I told the other kids to please help him out and ignore him so he could earn his free time. When the class was over, I asked him if the change of location helped. He said yes and he decided it was a good place for him to sit. Oh, if everything was just that easy!

I thought about taking it one step further. What about "reward the child *and* the good behavior"? It's not a novel idea. Teachers do it all the time, as did I, but this was going to be a conscious effort to be consistent with a casual monitoring of the results. What I also wanted to know was where the child would fit into it. I decided to use the positive verbal approach and to bring myself into the equation. So I used a line I had heard before: "I like the way you…" The blank could be filled in with words like "sit," "work," "write," "think," et cetera. I added a check mark system for reinforcement. When the child or group of children did something good, they got a positive comment and a check mark. Here's how it works…

Check This Out

Science is far from my best subject area. It's always fascinated me, but my cognitive ability to grasp the skills needed for the process left me limited to fascination and not much more. However, I did take on subbing for a grammar school science class. I knew the teacher, and she always left the best sub plans for dullards like me. And how difficult could second-grade science be? Extremely difficult, I discovered...but the problem had little to do with the subject area. This class was a science experiment in itself—a group of probably very nice kids, but when mixed together, the chemistry of the class was close to explosive. All those wonderful plans went up in smoke and I had them sit there and copy the words from a worksheet onto a piece of paper. Yes, positively boring and probably digressing from all the behavior modifications I was normally able to implement, but no one is perfect and when push comes to shove, it was much more conducive to my immediate goal: control. As they copied away, each table of students received from me a piece of white paper. The better they followed the rules I had set down, the more "good checks" they would receive.

This seemed to hold the fort down pretty well except for one student. You know, the one who designs the day around sounding like nails scraping across one of those old blackboards. Kids like this get on your every last nerve until you start to have visions of the shower scene from *Psycho* and you're Bates—wild-eyed, gender-inappropriately dressed, and holding the knife. Enacting this vision would come under the category of punishing the child, so this is when you have to flick through the channels in your head to Mr. Rogers. No one could want to punish a child during Mr. Rogers. Once that is done, focusing on punishing bad behavior and rewarding good behavior is much easier.

What also made things easier was that his group wasn't happy with this kid's antics either, because he was greatly interfering with their own pursuit of checks. When it comes to check denial, it's every man for himself. With the group's support, I was able to move him and his behavior to an isolated area. I gave him his white piece of paper to get his own checks and prayed he would do something other than crossing his arms and slumping in his chair so that I could show him I was really rooting for him to do well. After about five minutes, he finally wrote his name across the top of the paper. Not much to go on, but I grabbed the opportunity. I stood over him, complimenting his perfect penmanship, and gave him two checks for it. I could do this and mean it, because when it's just the behavior that's being focused on and not the child, you can leap from Norman Bates to Mr. Rogers pretty quickly.

The bottom line was that this child became the diligent little worker, not only copying the material but making each letter perfectly. He was the Michelangelo of penmanship. By the end of class, he was the proud owner of perfectly neat work, seven checks, and all the compliments I had lavished upon him. When the teacher came to collect the kids, the boy walked up to me, tightly grasping the paper like a prize, and politely asked if he could keep it. He wanted to take it home and show his mother his good work checks. I told him he earned those checks and he could keep them. He smiled this huge smile and then hugged me before running over to the linc and showing his teacher his checks. It was just a scrap of paper with some marks on it, yet he treated it like a winning lotto ticket. Maybe for him, it was. Maybe for him, it was the first time he got something for showing good behavior.

What amazed me, as I watched him leave the room waving good-bye to me, is that forty-five minutes earlier he had been my worst nightmare. Now I really liked the kid. He sprouted angel wings and a halo over seven little marks on a paper. I think it is the right way to go: punish the behavior and not the child. Think of it as "nothing personal." The child is not bad, only the behavior is. I learned something even more valuable, too. When you reward the behavior, most children take it very personally and they not only feel good about themselves, they feel good about you too. At least this little guy did.

P.S., two years later, I was at the same school presenting a special program I had developed on the environment and there he was. He remembered me and I remembered him—for all the right reasons.

Beats Yelling

There is a bit of a downside to the method. For one thing, like most everything, it doesn't work with every child or in every class. There are times when you just have to throw in the towel and Norman Bates cannot be ignored. However, it is more the exception than the rule. The other downside to being nice all day is it is exhausting. Is it worth it? Well, I think one sixth grader helped me sum that up. He was in a middle school computer class. I had taken the substitute job because the previous science teacher was now teaching this class and followed through on great plans. I used the check method in this class too and enticed the students a bit more by having them earn tickets for the school store. As they worked on their computers, I walked around writing check marks on each child's paper, expressing reinforcing comments. Some students would actually say "Thank you," to which I would answer, "You're welcome. Nice manners!" It became contagious and pretty soon most students were saying "Thank you." This was really sweet, but it got a bit tediously redundant with the "You're welcome. Nice manners." I actually think they were taking bets to see if I would keep saying it to each and every one of them. Maybe it was all just a game to them and their way of making me suffer persecution by redundancy.

On what seemed like my six-hundredth "You're welcome. Nice manners," one boy said, "Aren't you sick of saying that?"

I wanted to scream, "Sick to death!" I didn't want to lie and say "No, I just love it." He would have known I was lying. So I looked at him, shrugged my shoulders, and told him the truth: "Beats yelling."

He thought about that for a second, nodded his head, and responded, "Yeah, it does," and he added, "Thanks."

To which I responded, "You're welcome. Nice manners."

5

It's Everybody's Business

Hell's Kitchen

During my college years, I was a part-time waitress. Now, there's a job that is highly underrated. It was one of those off-the-highway-family-sit-and-enjoy-a-good meal restaurants. The head waitress there was a real pro who hated the sight of part-time college students. She considered them sloppy, amateur snobs; ergo, she hated me. She did everything she could to make my life and the other students' lives miserable by pointing out everything she felt we were doing wrong. I really didn't need this, but was smart enough to know that I couldn't fight her on it. I decided to try a different approach.

One day she was standing next to me while we both waited for our tables to clear. I told her I wanted to thank her. Boy, did that get her attention. "For what?" she asked, looking at me from the top of her flared-tip rhinestone glasses. I told her that I would never be as good a waitress as she was (which was definitely the truth) and yet she always took time to point out what I was doing wrong to help me improve. That last part was a big stretch of the truth. I think half of her felt sorry for me for being so stupid. The other half felt like I had plumped up her feathers. She was being acknowledged for her work being important and pristine. I think she had a preconceived notion that the college students looked down at her. Obviously, no one had bothered to tell her that some of our academic courses were easier than serving some of those food courses. It could be hell in that kitchen, not to mention some of the customers.

After that, she became not only my best ally, but a friend. The chip was off the shoulder. It made me think that being nice and acknowledging someone's worth can go a long way. Not only that, but now when she pointed out what I was doing wrong, I listened and I have to say I became a better waitress for it. Which leads me to the next part...

Everyone

Everyone I talk to nowadays is unhappy at work, and that is a mega-understatement. I don't just mean teachers. I mean everyone, in all types of jobs, from California to Connecticut, from entry-level to high-level positions. Everyone. One of the largest complaints isn't even about the amount of work, the lack of money, or the hours. It's the company's negative attitude and lack of appreciation and the fact that no matter what you do, it just wants more and more out of you. If work morale could be traded as a stock, we'd be in the second Great Depression. Even without the stock trading, the word "depression" fits. Workers are depressed, feeling undervalued and defeated in epidemic numbers. That line on the graph just dove to the bottom. How is that good for business? It's not. "You'd think once in a while they could say please or thank you," is like a mantra

I hear from all. It's not like it costs anything to say it. It's not going to put a dent in the budget.

What ever happened to those antiquated social graces that had once been monotonously pounded into our vocabulary? Where did being nice go? Maybe business executives should have to take a social etiquette course and learn how to maintain a positive attitude. Or maybe they should have to sit in a school classroom and take a few pointers from the teacher, who should be sainted for patience. An argument business higher-ups might make is their jobs have much more pressure and stress than other jobs and more is riding on their performance. Okay, maybe arguing this point is for another day, but if that's the case then I reiterate: maybe they should sit in a school classroom.

Let's take a common sense approach. A "you catch more bees with honey" approach. When going over a written assignment with a student, be it for grammar or content, my method (and that of many others) is to point out what the student did right first. "Wow, I really like the way you used that word." "Wow, you really have some suspense going on here." "Wow, you really described that perfectly. I can actually see it." Okay, you can leave out all the "wows," but you get the point. Same thing when correcting, say, students' math papers: mark all the items they get correct first, or say how many they got right instead of how many they got wrong.

Look for what is good first. Why? You may ask. Apart from the fact that the kids are strutting back to their desks instead of slumping back, they are now "with" you, not "against" you. They feel good about themselves because you complimented them and they feel good about you because you noticed "the good stuff." There could be about seventy-five more reasons, which I'll leave out and shoot for brevity, but there is something to say about how it makes you lighten up, too. I mean, you may even find yourself smiling when saying all these simpatico things. Being nice is just as contagious as being miserable.

Once that is done, you start in on what needs to be fixed. How to make the work *better* has a more amicable ring than how to make it *good*. It's already good; the pressure's off, the attitude and anger is put aside, the hard part is done, and the rest is touch-up. Students have confidence in what they do correctly and can repeat it with ease next time while focusing only on what's still an issue. Things are clearer to them. With clarity and confidence comes a higher turnout in performance. Think of that old saying, "might makes right," and change it to "right makes might."

The students have one more motivation factor too: you. They are more willing to listen because you're an ally, not an adversary. It also works wonders on the child who just doesn't want to do anything. We all have those, even in the grown-up workforce. When kids like that start complaining about you being unfair, instead of a cheerleading team of their peers, they get a shrug and are ignored. So these bad apples either shape up or shut up (or, if they're adults, ship out).

Back to the business world of bosses (even the bosses of teachers): do what teachers do. Add a few "pleases" and "thank-yous" and throw in a smile, and productivity may be on the rise. Get some of the positive attitude and politeness into that portfolio and profit margin. It's good for the soul, good for the spirit, and most important, good for business. And isn't that what really matters? I'll let you answer that.

PART III

Extracurricular Activities

*

From "howdy duty" to au revoir, not all the work is restricted to the classroom.

6
In-School Duties

The Tale of Two Duties

Every teacher can usually count on some extra duties. Every school has a different way of doing them. Most teachers can count on having a door duty, a bus duty, and possibly hall duty and lunch duty. In the school where I taught, we had two: morning door duty and bus duty. Victor Hugo said, "He who opens a school door, closes a prison." I assume he was the reason we got door duty.

These are times, however, when a more casual relationship can move between teacher and student. For door duty, I tried to learn to say hello in all the students' first languages. I now could do a "meet and greet" in Middle Eastern countries, Spanish-speaking countries, Tibet, and Ghana. During bus duty I would have each student stop before getting on, then thank him or her for waiting and say good-bye in French, Italian, or the Middle English (Anglo-French) "adieu." Every occasion can be used as a learning experience for all of us. At least, that's how I liked to look at it.

The younger students love to share some piece of personal information at these times—things like "I got a puppy!" or "My father's home from jail." Usually, teachers learn to give the same smile to both types of comments and to respond with "That's wonderful." These times can also bring some uncomfortable situations.

Howdy Duty

Once when I walked out for "howdy duty" (a school joke about "morning door duty") at the fifth grade door, standing among my students were two high school kids. I could have ignored that, except for the fact that they were kissing with full tongue and humping each other in a vertical position. Not only that, but every fifth-grader made sure I spotted them. As if I could have missed it.

I had to interrupt their moment of passion. I was, of course, met with protests such as, "What, what'd I do?"

I had to respond, "Well, if you don't know, then you're obviously too young to be doing it." All fifth-grade eyes were on me as I looked up at these two hormonal youths, trying to get them to vacate the premises.

They finally began a slow retreat from the school yard, not without yelling the word "bitch" accompanied by other equally uncomplimentary words. I pretended not to hear it. I mean, the day really hadn't even started yet and I was already developing fourth-period fatigue. I figured by this time some students were already placing bets on who was going to leave winning. A group of them were more than happy to repeat the teenagers' final comment. Surrounded by wide-eyed anticipation, I smiled at the students, waved my hand in the air and with a nonchalant bravado said, "Oh, coming from them, I take it as a compliment." It took a few moments for them to digest the meaning of this and then they smiled in approval, put thumbs up, and a few girls asked me to repeat what I had said so they could use it in their own repertoire of insult comebacks. Charles Dickens says in *Hard Times* that "There is a wisdom of the head, and a wisdom of the heart," but there is also a wisdom in a quick and clever comeback. I'm sure he meant to include that.

Bus Duty

Crapy

Howdy Duty Time is nothing compared to bus duty. While standing with my bus line of second and third graders, one girl, waving a piece of paper in her hand, called out to me that the boy in front of her had used a swear word. She had proof. It was written on the paper. I took the paper and examined its contents while the girl stood firm with her arms crossed and the boy tried to muster up a look of defiance. I was trying harder not to laugh as I read the offending line: "You look crapy."

I folded the note and addressed them both. "First of all, this is not a swear word. It is a vulgar word and shouldn't be used, but it's not a swear word." I repeated this, then addressed just the boy. "Second of all, you spelled 'crappy' wrong. You need to double the consonant 'p' to make the 'a' short."

This was obviously not the response he was expecting. His defiance melted to a confused relief. "Thanks," he said. "I'll remember that." I gave him a hard "teacher" look. He got the point. "I won't use it again, though." Once he gave the obligatory apology to the girl, I shook my head, stuffed the note in my pocket, and walked away.

The walk to the bus went smoothly. Everyone was very polite in line and all good-byes were said in French, Italian and Adieu. As I headed for my car, I thought, in a moment of complete fantasy, about how easy it would be to teach reading and spelling using swear words, especially the short vowel sounds. It's wrong, of course, very wrong, absolutely out of the question, and I would never do it under any circumstances. Well, I thought, as I slammed my car door shut, I'll skip the road less traveled and just keep on plowing through all the old, wearisome methods. It's a far, far better thing I do, but I'll bet those test scores would have skyrocketed.

The Sorority of Strangers

Along with swear words and vulgar words, there are the taboo words. The ones that are so crude you just cringe. They are the bottom-feeders of vocabulary. Most of them are racial, cultural, or ethnic slurs. They are forbidden in the classroom, on field trips, in assemblies, or at any other organized, teacher-run activity. There's no way to determine at what age or exactly at which of many places a student may have picked up one of these rude, ignorant, offensive, and nauseating colloquialisms.

I had a kindergarten and first-grade bus line one year. My bus helper was a great girl from fifth grade. She was wonderful with the younger children, yet she could be firm and gained their respect, along with mine. Sometimes I forgot she was a student and thought of her more as a peer.

In this bus line, most of my attention went to one small kindergarten girl. She was cute as a button, always smiling, and unfortunately had no idea of what the word "boundaries" meant. Instead of spending the entire bus time correcting her behavior,

I decide to make her my special line helper. This meant she would walk in front with me and hold my hand to confirm her status. She liked this idea and would swing my arm back and forth as she skipped beside me.

While waiting outside for the bus on a lovely day, I had all the kids lined up against the wall. I noticed that my arm was no longer swinging and my little helper's feet had stopped moving in place. I looked at her and saw a serious, quizzical look on her face. I knew a question was coming, but never in my wildest dreams would I have been ready for this one. "Miss Iaccarino," she said, "my mama says that all white people are niggers. Is that true?" This was a lose-lose question. I couldn't even think of an answer. Both my little special helper and my fifth-grade helper were black, which made it even more impossible to answer. Of course, my first reaction would have been to give a stern reprimand for using the 'n' word. I also knew that since she had no idea of the word's negative power, I'd have to take the opportunity to explain. This was a place I didn't want to be going. Answering the original question was already an impossibly rocky road to cross.

I looked at my fifth-grade helper for some direction, but she had the same look on her face that I did—pure panic, complete macabre awe, and for reasons neither one of us could understand, embarrassment. The blonde-haired, blue-eyed classmate standing behind my questioner in line had heard the query and thought he would offer assistance. Placing his index finger on his chin, he commented, "I don't think so. I think all white people are Negroes and all black people are niggers." Ouch! I'm dying here and there's no bus in sight to rescue me.

Now three sets of wide eyes were looking at me: my little helper, the boy, and my fifth-grade helper. I took a deep breath and, mustering up all my ability to fake calm naiveté, I said, "Well, all I know is that we are all human beings, which means we are all the same. As far as the other stuff, I think you're going to have to talk that over with your mom." Thank God and the guardian angel of bus lines, the two little ones nodded their heads, showing they accepted my answer. My fifth-grade helper had pure relief on her face and gave me a thumb up. "Oh, look!" I called out. "The bus is here!"

I practically sprinted the line over to its waiting, open doors. When all but my fifth-grade helper were aboard, I put my hand on her shoulder to signal her to wait. Our camaraderie was confirmed by the lingering look of embarrassment on our faces. "That was a good answer," she said.

"Thank you," I answered, then added, "And that conversation never really took place, right?" We both knew that I would have to report it, but we really just wanted it to go away.

"What conversation?" She smiled and we gave each other a hug, because we were both just human beings, and that's the way we liked it. It made life and language so much simpler and seemed to give more power to what was really significant than the power of a six-letter word.

Dah Bell! Dah Bell!

I am, as you can tell, a fan of Victor Hugo, so I talked one of the fourth-grade teachers into letting me come in and teach the students about *The Hunchback of Notre Dame.* I would tell them about the story, what life was like during Quasimodo's time and then show them the ancient, black-and-white 1939 movie starring Charles Laughton. One student asked me why the class had to learn about these old stories. I gave a rather lengthy lecture about the value of the classics and how they are timeless. He didn't look all that convinced even when I was done.

I had the same boy as my bus helper at the second-grade wing. We were standing together watching the children in line when the bell for final dismissal rang. We whipped our hands over our ears, since we were standing right under the bell. The second the noise ended, I dropped my shoulder down, lowered my neck, and swung my arm to do my best Quasimodo impersonation. I looked at my helper and said "Dah bell! Dah bell!"

The children in line thought I had just lost my mind, but the boy cracked up laughing. "I got it!" he said, as he continued to laugh and started his own hunchback arm swinging.

"And that's another reason why we study the classics," I confirmed. We all love being privy to a private joke, and we get to walk around like Quasimodo.

So, in keeping with the situation, let me say *salam alaykum, hola, tashi dele, ete-sen, arrivederci, au revoir,* and *adieu.*

What Stinks About Lunch

In my grammar school days when you came home from school to watch the black-and-white, rabbit-ear TV while wearing your Mickey Mouse ears, there was no such thing as a "hot lunch." (A "breakfast program" usually meant a Saturday-morning cartoon.) You would be packed off for the day with your paper bag or metal lunchbox and thermos that sat in the coatroom until the hour when you sat in silence and ate the contents. You also had the choice of walking the mile and a half home to eat there. And I'll bet you're wondering now if Laura Ingalls Wilder was my first-grade teacher, which really isn't that funny.

Obviously, and thank goodness, there have been many changes since those days, which really weren't all that long ago, honest. We have made considerable progress, but in the process, we have become inundated with processed food. It is the prescribed diet for just about every school system, and it literally and figuratively stinks—not to mention that it has been shown to be incredibly unhealthy. Thankfully, some systems are really making attempts to excise the prefab foodstuff. You really don't need a team of scientists, biologists, and nutritionists to tell you that this is the right way to go; all you have to do is go into a school and work in the lunchroom. I really think those lunch ladies wear those required hygienic plastic gloves to protect themselves from touching the food.

An Apple a Day

Luckily, the kids throw half of it out. Everything that isn't eaten goes into the trash; that is the cardinal law. I did feel bad about the apples that were eventually included on the menu. It was a bold move to actually include fruit. I asked once if I could take the apples the kids didn't eat for the deer in my backyard. I had a huge four-pointer buck who just loved them and it wasn't like the school was going to use them for great compost. They were headed for the hell of a chemical, Styrofoam, and plastic dump. Separation of church, state, and education aside, you don't need a religion to understand that throwing these apples out is an environmental sin.

I checked with the principal about taking the apples and she had no problem with it, except that she was not the god of the lunchroom. Somewhere it was written in the bible of food service that the apples had to go. Maybe it went back to Adam and Eve and the whole apple-and-serpent situation.

You know that story. Maybe somewhere, someone had been sued for saving apples. The harder I tried to get the apples using common sense, the more opposition I got. So the more persistent I became.

I decided to go undercover. I casually mentioned the issue to some of the students. They liked deer and decided to help by sneaking their apples out and spreading the word to their friends. I would go into my room after lunch and find a line of apples on my desk. I was the only teacher in the school that students were giving apples to, and I have to say, some of the other staff were a bit jealous. If they only knew!

One of the lunch ladies, who had a heart, would put some extra aside and would turn her head when I went in to collect them. I told a friend in another school and she had a little talk with some of the kids in her lunchroom. I would come home and find a bag of apples on my back steps. Some had bites in them, but I didn't think Buck and the other deer would mind.

I never in my wildest dreams thought I would be involved in the covert action of saving apples. I was proud of my little army of brave souls. After washing off the pesticides I would head out to the yard and Buck. I smiled as he and some of the buddies he brought along ate contraband fruit. I did break one of the thirteen-plus commandments of the lunch program, and I accepted responsibility for it. Like Harry Truman, my motto is "the buck stops here"—literally and figuratively speaking, of course.

A Moral Dilemma Menu

While subbing in middle school, I had lunch duty. The only thing that was more painful than the noise was seeing the food the kids were given to eat. To add insult to injury, there were vending machines with soda, potato chips, and other plastic-wrapped junk items. One of my favorite homeroom students raised her hand to call me over. She requested permission to go to the vending machine for some popcorn. I was in a real quagmire as I saw the uneaten hot dog sitting on her plate. "The rule is," I told her, "your plate has to be empty before you can go to the machines."

"But I can't eat this," she answered as we both stared down at the dog in disgust.

"Oh, God, I'd never eat that either. It's repulsive."

"You wouldn't?" she questioned, looking surprised.

"Yuck! I'd starve first." I guess I should have been a bit more tactful, but I couldn't muster up that many acting skills.

"So I can get the popcorn?" she asked, thinking this was a no brainer.

This is the part where it got tricky. There was a real moral dilemma here. The popcorn had to be better for her to eat than the hot dog, though I did worry about the GMOs. It was a case of bad—the popcorn—to worse: the hotdog. I decided to speak in code. "The rule is—" I spoke very slowly—"that your dish has to be clean before I let you go to the vending machine. Now, I'm going to walk away. You can eat the hot dog. You can break it up and stick it under your napkin or in your empty milk carton. But I can't let you go until the dish is empty."

She looked like she understood, but couldn't believe I would tell her to do something like that. I did feel a bit like Pontius Pilate, washing my hands of the whole affair, but I was going with my gut and my gut was telling me there was no way I was going to force her to eat the processed mass of meat by-products, ammonia, hormones, antibiotics, chemicals, *and* GMOs. It was the lesser of the two evils.

Moments later, her hand went up. I returned and the plate was empty. I lifted the napkin by the side of the plate, and to my relief, tiny bits of hot dog and bun were mashed together in the hiding place. "Well," I said, smiling and nodding to her in approval, "Your plate is empty. You can go to the vending machine."

On her way back, I called her aside and told her that this was between us and that she really shouldn't do it again with another teacher. Her response was, "I'm seriously thinking of bringing in my own lunch from home."

"I love the way you think," I told her. I knew I liked her for a reason.

I almost became nostalgic for that black-and-white TV, those Mickey Mouse ears, and paper bag lunches, but I'd miss my movies on demand, all the "i" electronics, spell check and the remote car starter. If only we could have the best of both worlds.

7
Parent Conferences

I like the way e-mail has made its way into the school systems. Now teachers can e-mail parents the homework for the night, midterm grades, a message about any issue that arose that day, notification of events coming up. It's an easier and more efficient way to communicate with parents. There is, however, nothing like a parent conference. It's that face-to-face encounter that really forms the relationship, be it a good one or not. A lot can be said about using a face-to-face, body-language, human encounter to learn about the child and his or her folks. The downside is that communication isn't really completely free flowing in a conference because teachers have to watch what they say—and so do parents, for that matter. There is no *insert* or *delete* like in e-mail. The upsides? You don't have to worry about spell check missing one of those educational six-syllable words, and once you get to know the parents and they're with you on things, you can relax the formality vernacular.

I have met some of the nicest people I know during conferences, and they deserve to be mentioned. Some of the parents I met I still keep in contact with me even though their child has gone off to college. Some have even become friends. These are the people who may not always agree with you and may ask a lot of questions, but it all comes from a genuine concern about their child. Their arguments are sound and their questions good, and they are always willing to listen and keep an open mind.

When I first started teaching, I was in a program where I could see a student from kindergarten through the fifth grade. After a few years, parent conferences could become more of a social event—a "how's the family?" kind of meeting. Everyone talked freely, language was informal, and confidences were shared. We were a team and it made up for all the other awful parent conferences I'd had to sit through.

Speaking in Code

There was one mother who I got to know well and liked. She would tell me that she understood why her daughter got on my nerves. Actually, she started our first conference with "I'll bet my daughter gets on your nerves…" There was no point in denying it. Some lies are just too transparent. She said it was okay, her child got on her nerves all the time. As our conferences went on—we had more than just the required sum, including frequent phone calls—she stated that if I felt I needed to haul off and give her daughter a good slap once in a while, she would totally understand.

Did I report her to Child Services? I wouldn't think of it. I might have if I had just met her, but I knew her. I knew she loved her child. There was a sense of pride in her voice and along with the irritating faults mentioned; the mom also mentioned the daughter's good qualities. She also followed through on any phone call I made. She made sure homework was done. The daughter respected and admired her mother. We even both took her daughter out to dinner as a reward for doing a good job. The comment was just the mother's way of saying that she understood her daughter was difficult and that she appreciated me having patience with her and even liking her. She knew I would never hit her child, and I knew she wouldn't either. Just to put minds to rest, the child never came in bruised, and when asked, she let me know with words I won't repeat that she was shocked I could ever think her mother would hit her.

I Hate My Mother

With the good comes the bad. That's just the way it is. One good meeting with a parent, and in walks another and up comes the bad. This particular one came with a mother whose daughter constantly stated that she hated her mother and that her mother hated her. This didn't sound too far-fetched, since she was always dirty, and the classroom teacher and I had to provide her with a Halloween costume, field trip money, and snacks. Still, I felt that "hate" was such a strong word.

I was a bit anxious to meet the mother. She was one tough cookie with volumes of attitude. She walked in, announced who she was, sat down and said, "My daughter probably told you she hates me, which is fine because I hate her too."

My first reaction would have been to ask her to leave, go home, and enroll in a school that taught Motherhood 101. Since this wasn't really an option, I chose the second best approach. I lied. "No," I said with a perfectly straight face, "she told me she loves you very much." She looked surprised, maybe even a little guilty. It was short-lived. The girl ended up in foster care. Maybe she grew up and had a daughter. Maybe she went to a parent conference and told the teacher, "My daughter probably told you she hates me, which is fine because I hate her too." Hopefully, that teacher will lie too. Hopefully, it will make a difference somewhere along the line. We can only hope.

All in Due Time

The initial meet and greet is usually the most difficult for both parties. No one is sure what face they should put on. I remember my first experience with parent conferences. I was so prepared. I had documentation and had even practiced different pleasantly professional expressions in the mirror.

My first mom and dad walked in. I had a paper in front of me with a list of their son's learning disabilities. I made sure I stressed the fact that their son was smart. With tons of examples, I pontificated on what learning disabilities were, how they affected his learning, and what we were doing to help. The mother was sitting slightly behind the father. Her hands were tightly gripped together on her lap and her lips pressed together just as tightly. You could tell she had gotten the word from her husband to just sit there and shut up. He had his arms folded and occasionally nodded his head, as if he was listening and understood. When I was finished, the father finally spoke. "Okay," he said, moving closer to the desk and pointing his index finger down each item on the list. "Just tell me when this, this, this will go away."

Obviously, he hadn't been listening to a word I said. All my hard work and preparation went right over his head and out the window. I could just back up and start all over again, which seemed like an exercise in futility, or I could just give him what he wanted. "Well," I said, looking down at the paper and pointing to each item. "This should be gone by December third, around 2:42 p.m. This one I'd say will be gone on January fourteenth, around 6:36 a.m., and this one is done on April twelfth, I'd say between 4:55 and 5:05."

For everything this father seemed to lack, he did, thank goodness, have a good sense of humor. He smiled and said, "That was a stupid question, wasn't it?"

"Definitely," I answered. I saw his wife smile and nod her head. He seemed to relax and I explained everything one more time, except this time he listened and asked all the right questions. Fear and insecurity are probably the biggest learning disability we all have to overcome.

Klutz

It was a good thing that I was a pro at conferences when I made a complete idiot out of myself, which ended up saving the day. It was my first meeting with this particular mother. She just didn't want to accept the fact that her son had a learning disability. I was beating the dead horse with obvious examples, but she wasn't going to budge. I was down to saying that her son was clumsy and that it could be due in part to his specific disability. As I spoke, I stood and began to walk around the desk so I could sit next to her instead of across from her. I thought that lessening the physical distance between us might possibly help lessen the tension as well.

I took my second step and put my foot right into my purse, sending me halfway across my desk. I was lying on top of all the papers, my face inches from hers. I smiled and said, "And if anyone knows about clumsy, it's me." The two of us burst out laughing and the rest of the conference went great. Sometimes you just have to make an ass out of yourself before a parent is willing to trust in how scholarly you really are.

So, to all those wonderful parents that I had the privilege to meet, I thank you. You are inspirational and not acknowledged enough for what you do. You do make a difference in your child's life and success.

8
Workshops

Workshops…we all have to go to them. Some are state authorized, some city authorized, some are about paperwork, some about teaching techniques, some about required programs to follow, and some are just informative. Whatever the case, teachers become the students and sit and listen. There were several I attended where I enthusiastically took notes and applied what I learned. In others, I practiced my doodling skills and updated my "to-do" list.

My least favorite workshops were the ones for the new required academic programs. Luckily, being special-ed, I was occasionally forgotten and not included. Usually, special-ed students were also forgotten, or the modifications for them were insipid and lumped every IEP student into one generic category. I chose to reciprocate equally and ignore their program as much as they ignored mine. To be fair, there was an occasional exception were I actually used the program with an open mind and a "Bravo!" for its creators.

There was one workshop I absolutely loved. My school got involved in an early-dropout prevention program. We not only had school meetings, we all piled on a bus and crossed state lines for a full-day observation of how it worked. We even met during the summer to work with the presenters to make changes that we felt would allow the program to work better in our school setting. They listened to our ideas, learned from our approaches, and validated what we did by adopting some of our changes into their program. They even put us in the book they published. Now, that's respect!

Shopping for What Works

What is a workshop but working on shopping around for ideas, materials, and techniques that make the teaching day successful? Shopping for these items is like shopping for clothes or even a car. Sometimes we go to the mall, sometimes we go to a local place for something unique and befitting our style. So, instead of (or even including) the large teacher workshops, what about "own-school" workshops where teachers present what they are doing that works (or even doesn't work) for them?

These small workshops would be like the clothes in that local store: distinctive to the area. What would be great about them is that there wouldn't have to be hours of prep, PowerPoint presentations, handouts, or graphs and diagrams documenting failure or success rates. We're going for small and intimate, short and sweet. We're not talking about a "brag-about" or "dump-on" session. It's not an ego contest. I'd say it is more like one of those morning meetings with the kids where everyone sits in a circle, greets the person next to them, goes over the day's events, weather, et cetera, and then shares an experience. Now skip the meet and greet, the etcetera, and go right to the sharing. That's the type of experience we're going for here.

All Set!

What can you learn at a "local" workshop? I learned some of the best and quickest ways to exchange information. When I was sitting in a second-grade class once, the teacher announced a change to a new subject. After the directions were given, she joyfully called out, "All set!"

The kids answered just as joyfully, "You bet!"

And you can bet they got right to task. Amazing. How simple! How easy! The best part is how long it takes the teacher to explain this to peers—what, maybe three minutes? Probably the shortest workshop presentation in history.

Four!

I watched a fifth-grade teacher use golf (his favorite game) to teach math. Not only were the students getting the math skills, they were becoming avid golf fans. I watched another teacher transform the most boring of skill reviews into exhilarating competition by whipping out an "easy button." (I went out and bought two of those buttons.) Most teachers have some variation of reward boards, jobs for the day, learning centers, pairing and sharing of groups. Most of these concepts originated in basic educational theory, but are tailored according to the teacher's style of presentation and how the class functions. In other words, the teacher bought a minivan (the general workshop), took it home, and with some fine tuning and bodywork transformed it into a high-speed, smooth-running sports car.

That's Okay

Sometimes there are things that work for one teacher that don't work for another, and that's okay. The thing is, we all have to understand the simple line "That's okay." Use it as a mantra. Say it each morning with three deep breaths as you enter the classroom. Try some new technique on your class, and if it doesn't fit the students' needs, just tell yourself "that's okay," and pass it on to someone else it might work for. The important part is that you tried it. Move on and try something else. Lighten up on yourself. It's not a reflection of how well you teach.

Think of your teaching technique as your favorite car. You're a good driver, you know that; your driving record proves it. Your teaching peer also has an outstanding driving record. The difference is, you are very comfortable in your Mini and he's pleased as punch in his SUV. He can tell you about all the wonders of the SUV and each aspect of its value. All of it can be absolutely true, but the SUV is just not for you, and that's okay.

I've watched some teachers use things that worked like a charm. I tried them and afterward, while the class either completely ignored me or looked at me like I had two heads, I thought, "Well, I've risen to a whole new level of ineptitude." I still passed it on to others, because it might work for someone else. I say that because I took three deep breaths and repeated, "That's okay."

The Tiger Sleeps Tonight

The best example I can think of for this principle is something I saw when a teacher was walking her class to a special area. The kids were starting to be a bit chatty, so she turned, placed one hand up to raise the two peace-sign fingers and with her other hand raised her index finger to her lips. There was complete and utter silence. "Wow," I thought, "that's for me." But it wasn't. I tried it once, got absolutely no acknowledgment from the students, and was left looking like a bad imitation of the Statue of Liberty. I took three deep breaths and said, "That's okay."

The next time I had a class marching off to the lunchroom, I told the kids as they stood lined up at the door that behind the line was a sleeping tiger. Yes, I actually said that, and I didn't stop there. I continued by saying that we didn't want to wake the sleeping tiger because tigers are very grouchy when they wake up and they growl, they claw, and they bite! I then smiled and winked, just in case there were any students in the group as gullible as I am who believe everything they are told. Well, maybe not everything.

I want to point out before you read the next part that I am a product of the old-time, whack-your-hand-with-a-ruler Catholic grammar school. So the story you are about to read is no reflection on the nuns of today. There are so many of them out there now doing so many great things. Just look at Mother Teresa. She had my vote for pope. Anyway, way, way back in grammar school I was told by a nun sitting near me in church that if I turned around to talk one more time, I would turn to salt. Oh, please! Whack my hand with that ruler, but don't insult my intelligence. I tested out this obvious fabrication by turning around to talk once more. I'm still here, which shows how well her method worked. I wonder if she took three breaths and said the mantra.

Unlike my past teacher, I waited for the entire class to show signs of understanding that I was making the tiger story up. It was just a game. Once that was accomplished, we marched off. If someone started talking, I turned and said, "I think I hear the tiger yawning..." or waking up, or growling—whatever worked with the class. Some of the students, especially the very young, really get into this and even walk on tiptoe. You might get, as I have, some students who feel above all this and give you an annoyed dirty look or are bad sports about playing this little game. I tend to ignore them. If they don't let up, I put them in the back of the line furthest away from me and closest to the tiger.

If you feel a hankering toward this approach, feel free to change to any sharp-toothed, spiky-clawed, or large-winged species of your choice. You can pick some fairy-tale four-legged villain or go for a popular, classical, or cartoon musical motif. If you think none of this will ever work for you, that's okay. Try the Statue of Liberty method; that's okay too.

Here's Looking at You

Some things you have to hear from a peer's own lips to believe it could even work. I remember one instance at Eco camp. I had broken my foot, so instead of walking with the group to a particular area, I had to drive. I stood watching as the forty or so happy campers walked toward me. They were chatting away. After all, it was camp. Some of the junior counselors, along with me, tried various ways (including saying "Shhhh!") to stop the talking at the beginning of the nature lecture. Nothing was working and my foot was throbbing, along with my head. All of sudden, I called out, "Okay, I'm going to look at the first group of you that I can't hear." Once said, I couldn't believe it had left my lips. I don't even think the grammar was quite correct, God forbid. The junior counselors had that questioning look on their faces too. What was most amazing was that the sound of voices came to a dull lull. So I continued. I pointed to a few campers at a time, looked directly at them, and said, "Good job. I'm looking at you!" Who would have thought that would work? I never would have. I'd even think twice, maybe even three times, if someone had told me to try it.

The bottom line is, large workshops on large-scale programs can be great, but they aren't always the answer. I personally go for the motto "Tell me what to teach, but don't tell me how to teach it." That's just me, though. What we get in large workshops can be incredibly useful—but even more useful if we can change it around a bit. You just don't know what is going to work, with which class, which school or even school system. You have to shop around, try some ideas on for size, and see what fits for you. For some schools, a workshop may be too big or too small, and that's okay—as long as you have the option to make some alterations. Maybe mandatory workshops should, at the end of each presentation, have everyone take three deep breaths and say "that's okay."

PART IV
Laws and Orders

*

Anything you say can be used against you.

9

LAWS AND THEIR SUITS

(And how they don't fit)

You Talkin' to Me?

Have you noticed how life is full of trade-offs? There was a time when teachers used to worry about which suit to wear to work; now we worry about what suit is going to be brought against us. We've just traded one kind of suit for another. When lawsuits were unheard of, wardrobe restrictions were a very serious thing back in the days of thirty-five-cents-a-gallon-of-gas-guzzling cars with no seat belts.

Remember uniforms? Some schools have actually gone back to uniforms and with that have seen an improvement in behavior and grades. I wore a uniform in grammar school and never appreciated it until I had to learn and participate in the dress codes of middle and high school. I traded off a bland, look-alike skirt and blouse for a uniform of acceptable labels and correct color coordination. That had to be the most scrutinizing and stressful code I'd ever had to adhere to.

Once out of college and when cigarette commercials were first banned from TV, I had to retire my bell-bottom jeans, flower-embroidered gauze shirts, and leather sandals and take up dresses, skirts, pressed blouses, an initialed circle pin to accessorize, stockings or tights, and a proper pair of pumps. I felt like Janis Joplin morphed into Mary Poppins longing for the Marlboro man.

I was perhaps feeling just that at the end of a chilly fall day as I headed for my Ford Fairlane in the school parking lot. Dressed in my suitable attire of sweater, skirt, tights, long tailored coat and matching scarf, I walked slumped over with the weight of my purse, briefcase, and a very long day. Parked two rows before my car stood a man around my age. He was leaning his head into the driver's-side window where he was wrapping his lips around the semi-naked breasts of the woman behind the wheel.

I prayed she wasn't killing time while waiting to do her motherly duty of picking up her child. I decided not to even try to guess what *he* was killing time for. Then my thoughts turned to the possible child that might be hers and what he or she would think when arriving at the car. My biggest fear was that the child would think this was perfectly normal, and I really didn't want to be there to find out. Then the guy came up for air and spotted me. Even worse, he started talking to me. "Hey, lady, you a teach? Yah look like a teach. Huh, you a teach? Yah look like a teach."

I suppose I could have seen this as an opportunity to introduce a basic grammar lesson. Or I could have ignored him, gone to my car, and banged my head against the steering wheel. But he was looking me up and down as I walked in my appropriate apparel, laughing smugly as if his repetitive, one-syllable jabber could be perceived as clever and witty rhetoric. Though my wardrobe restrictions were as tight as any 1950s girdle, what I was allowed to say at that time was one step above bra burning.

I was angry, annoyed, disgusted, and repulsed, to put it mildly, by his treatment of this woman and also of me. I also felt a bit threatened, which calls up the natural choice between fight or flight. I chose the former. My weapon of choice was words, sharp and to the point. So I responded in a terminology appropriate to the recipient that would not be open to misinterpretation. I stopped for one brief moment, looked him up and down with a disapproving teacher look, and in my most professional voice I said, "You, sir, look like an asshole." His jaw dropped, which at least stopped him from licking flesh or talking. He was disarmed, at least for the moment. I figured the biggest lesson he learned here was not to judge a book—or a woman—by its (or her) cover. Of course, now I can wear pants (even jeans) to school, but my lips are sewn shut. That's the trade-off. It's a high price to pay for a pair of pants.

In this century, I don't worry about what's in TV commercials. I can just fast-forward past them all. My energy-efficient car equipped with seat belts and air bags now costs four dollars and upward per gallon to fill. *Happy Days* came and went, and so did my worry about parking lot rage. As I said, I'm dressed like the masses now. Not to mention, people like him just don't bother me anymore. What does bother me are the insecurities that come from educational restrictions, a girdle called a lawsuit, that causes uncertainty in decision making and an inner conflict between approach and avoidance when dealing with students. It's like the new dress code is a required albatross around everyone's neck. That bird can get pretty heavy and weigh you down and cloud your quick decision-making faculties in a delicate situation.

Which Way Do I Go? Which Way Do I Go?

Years later, wearing my cashmere sweater and jeans, I was doing a day of retirement subbing in a first grade. The kids were adorable. One boy in particular had a bright smile and a lively nature. He also had a variety of imaginary acquaintances and a personal aide to help him through the day. Most of the day moved by without incident, except when he returned from music. The aide was waiting in the classroom and I was leading the troops back in there. I had the boy at the front of the line with me, holding his hand to make sure I could keep him safe if any of his "associates" appeared.

We were just by a door that led outside when he started pulling away from me, heading for the exit. I politely told him that he had to come with us back into the room. He was adamant about going outside because the goblins were there and he needed to hear what they were saying. Okay, so I have twenty-five little first graders plus one goblin catcher that I am supposed to return to the room safely. Do I force him back into the room? No, that leaves me open to a lawsuit. Do I ignore him and let him run out? No, that leaves me open to a lawsuit. Do I ignore the other twenty-five kids and take a walk with him outside to converse with his imaginary friend? No, that leaves me open to yet another lawsuit.

With all this in mind, I took the only option I felt I had left, which was to leap into the land of fiction. So I told him that he didn't want to go now because he wouldn't hear them very well. I told him that goblins can be heard better at night when it was dark. "So," I said, "tonight when you're home and it's dark out, don't go outside, but stay by a window and you'll be able to hear them perfectly." I had his undivided attention and probably a new respect due to my familiarity with the culture of goblins.

"Really!" he exclaimed, positioning himself closer to me and not pulling away. I gave him my Scout's-honor signal and he obediently returned to the classroom, happily anticipating nightfall. Yes, I did feel a bit guilty, but sometimes you just have to do what it takes to make things work. I was also pretty sure there were no lawsuits about giving directions on how to best talk to goblins, though you can never be *too* sure. Those lawsuits can get pretty spooky. Makes me think longingly of those proper pumps and circle pin.

The Gag Law

If you are a parent who is taking the time to read this book, then I'm not talking about your child here. The child I'm talking about in this section is no-holds-barred, no ifs, ands, or buts, The Bully. The one who thinks that acting like an idiot (is that an appropriate word?) is bravado, who constantly seeks attention by being oppositional (I know *that* is a politically correct word), and who harasses and terrifies for the fun of it. I'm referring to the chronic (yuck) "behavioral" student. These kids are the envelope-pushers of rude behavior, defiance, and challenging authority. We all know them. Luckily, some of their behavior is only a temporary stage, usually linked with raging hormones.

Bullies are nothing new. They go at least as far back as one-room school houses and blackboards (which were, by the way, much easier to keep clean than whiteboards. Chalk is very underrated. But that's another story). Something else that has disappeared, just like chalk, is school power. Power is one of those "sensitive" words. Power can be preceded by such words as "abuse of" and "excessive." The balance of power between school and parents is actually very important, but the scales are tipping now way off base. The sad part is, they aren't even tipping toward parents. Lady Justice has grown a third arm: some mutation caused by the environmental pollution of power that is the muscle for the rights of the bully. Lady Justice's blindfold has slipped down and is no longer hiding her eyes but concealing her mouth. She, along with teachers and parents who are trying to do their jobs for the youths assigned to their care, is choking on the gag law and worst of all, paying for it too.

Freedom of speech, protected by the First Amendment in the Bill of Rights, used to be held in the highest esteem in this country, probably right up there with "All men are created equal." (It has been noted that, at the time of its writing, "All men are created equal" really meant only white males who owned land. Still, for the times, it was a great stride in the race toward rights, liberty, and the pursuit of happiness.) In the realm of educational freedom of speech, there is the good, the bad, and the inappropriate. The definitions of good and bad have remained fairly consistent throughout the centuries. "Inappropriate" changes according to the various mores of the time, is left to interpretation, and gives rise to a wide array of lawsuits. Educationally speaking, we have been cut off from some of our rights and liberties with two words: "frivolous lawsuit."

Frivolous lawsuits protect the rights of the bully. They even protect parents who want to act like bullies. Want to know where a large percentage of those ridiculous school rules come from? They come from the financial bullies of adulthood. These are the parents who torment the school system and think they can make an easy buck by suing. Win or lose the suit, the school system pays. As a good parent and taxpayer, do you really want your money and the time of teachers and administrators being spent this way? Do you really want more ludicrous restrictions on you and your child and teachers when all you are looking for is a safe place for your child to get a good education? Remember, we're not talking about genuine lawsuits. We're talking thoughtless, silly, negligent, insipid, inconsiderate, and selfish lawsuits, and if the shoe fits...well, you know the rest. Or do you? Check out this pair of shoes.

A mother sent her second grader off to school wearing a cute dress and a pair of brand-new, patent leather shoes. The girl fell in the school yard during lunch recess. She had been playing a game with her friends when she slid on her shiny new soles and landed on the pavement, hurting her knee. A few days later, the parents started a lawsuit against the school for negligence. The suit named the principal, who had been at an obligatory meeting, the girl's teacher, who was out of the building during her lunch break, and the lunchroom staff, who were watching twenty-plus other students and didn't have time to check the bottoms of all their shoes.

I thought perhaps that the parents should have been sued for neglecting to scuff the bottoms of the shoes before sending the child off to school. I mean, everyone knows you take that old emery board out and give the bottoms a good once-over before putting shoes on. Duh! Unfortunately, no one asked me what I thought.

I don't know if the parents won the lawsuit, but nevertheless, the school system had to pay out money from tax dollars for its legal fees. To prevent this from happening again, the school passed a rule that no patent leather shoes could be worn to school. The only other time I heard of the banning of patent leather shoes was eons ago in the days of rotary phones when some Catholic schools banned girls from wearing them to dances. It seems that the boys could see what was up the girls' skirts from the reflection on the shoes. Anyway, since the case at hand has nothing to do with frivolous sexual misconduct, I'm surprised that the parents didn't turn around and sue the school for infringing on their child's wardrobe rights. Actually, I thought that the parents would have made out better suing the shoe company, but unfortunately, they never asked me what I thought about this either. I also think it would be a great idea if the parents and school system could sue these financial bullies for harassment, financial hardship, and assault for making us choke on the gag law. That could be just frivolous enough to work!

Bully for You!

There is nothing frivolous, however, about the classroom bully's behavior. These kids are dangerous and they come to school knowing their rights to be bullies. They are armed with those deadly words, "You can't touch me. You can't say that to me. You can't make me sit down, be quiet, stop swearing, or stop persecuting the kid next to me, because I'll sue you." At this point, teachers have to surrender, develop an unsurpassed evil eye, or call for a higher-up. They know the kid can sue and they know the administration doesn't have their backs. In fact, it is also questionable whether anybody has anyone's back. It pretty much leaves everyone watching their own backs, which can lead to many a stiff neck. If you find this hard to believe, then I suggest you become a substitute teacher for no less than two weeks. I also suggest that you include in your packed lunch a bottle of aspirin, some deep breathing exercise tapes, and earplugs, but bring nothing sharp that could be used as a weapon. Ego armor would be good, but not always easy to find. Bring bandages, because you'll spend a lot of time biting your tongue. Make sure you wear boots too, because you'll be walking on eggs most of the day and that can get very messy. Oh, and don't forget that neck brace.

In fairness, a bully does have a right to an education. We have to believe that somewhere trapped beneath the shenanigans and attitude is a model student that wants to come out. We should be guiding bullies in the direction of finding the model student within, not teaching them the power vocabulary that encourages them to remain bullies. We could try tough love, but we'd have to change the "tough" part, which sounds too violent and may be lawsuit material.

What about the children who want to learn and the teacher who wants to teach? Their day is constantly interrupted. Stress and tension hang in the room. Most important, their time for free education is being lost and given over to a few bad-behavior kids whom the teacher constantly has to address. The bottom line is that the bully is willfully denying those other students their rights under federal law to a free education. That bully is stealing their education, in part, and possibly opportunities for a better future. I'm sure somewhere there is correct legalese for the above rather high-pitched statement. I think you get the idea. It's time for parents to take a stand. It's time for parents to skip right past the school, take the power away from the bully, and save their tax dollars. It is time for them to give their children and the teacher the muscle they need to defeat the bully. Bottom line: if the teacher can't talk, money can.

It's easy and also virtually very simple. If that bad-behavior student stands in defiance, using four-letter words, cops a cocky attitude, sets the stage for belligerence and violence and smugly announces, "You can't stop me. I'll sue you," or anything along those lines that I can't repeat There is no need to disrupt the lesson. No need to argue, act as referee, psychologist, or police. No need for those students who want peace, quiet, and their right to learn to feel threatened or defenseless. If we have to live with the gag, let's pass it along. Let's use it to our advantage. Instead, the class and the teacher face the bully and their lawsuit-happy parents and call out in one voice, "Class-action suit!" It literally is a "class action" and not at all frivolous. I mean really, not at all frivolous.

10
And Orders

There are all kinds of order. There's the kind that is a command, like in the army. There's the kind that you give the waiter at a restaurant and the kind that has to do with sequence, like number order. There's also the kind that has to do with keeping peace and running things efficiently. We love order, especially in schools. Order makes everything neat and tidy. With order, a system runs smoothly. The problem is, one system of order does not necessarily fit every school system—or for that matter, every organization that functions within a school system. This is usually due to the arrangement of the most important element, the students, and the limited, preconceived perception that everyone else's situation should fit our own sense of order. Hard to follow? Here's an example.

Theory of Relativity

A very good friend of mine lives in a school district with large lawns and one-family houses. It's a great little town; I used to live there. She called me one night for advice about her son, who was a second-grade student at the time. It seemed that his school wanted to have an early intervention meeting concerning him. I was surprised. I knew her son well and I had never spotted any type of learning disability or educational lagsging. The problem, she stated, was that when he did his written work he was very slow and never finished on time. The reason, she explained was that he was a perfectionist. If he wrote a letter B, for instance, and it didn't come out flawlessly, he would erase and rewrite it until it was letter-perfect. This concerned his teacher, who called the meeting. My friend asked me, "What would your school do about something like this?"

I answered, "We'd put him in the gifted program."

It's all relative. Was her school overreacting? Would our school be negligent if we didn't call a meeting about something like this? Think about it. A child who could be considered for special-ed assistance in one school system could be worthy of praise in another. If her son had been in our school system, he would feel that he was doing an excellent job and feel confident and pleased. In the other school district, he now felt that there was something wrong with him, and his opinion of himself and his confidence would dwindle.

So here we have the same child with the same issue, and two different outcomes for the child. As I said, it's all relative. If only we could find that perfect theory of relativity for education. Where is Einstein when you need him? Speaking of Einstein, rumor has it that he had some type of learning disability. Where would we have placed him on the educational scale of success stories?

The Hierarchy Order of Acronyms (THOOA)

I've probably been called many things during my teaching career, especially with a last name like mine, but one of my favorites was "Ms. Acronym." I was dubbed this by a sixth-grade student I had worked with during English class. (I dread to think what I would have been called if I had had him during science—perhaps "Ms. H2O" or "Ms. "CO2.") Everything these days seems riddled with endless initialisms and/or acronyms. Have you checked your e-mail, Facebook account, or text messages lately? FWIW (for what's it's worth), it's almost impossible to find a complete word in any of them, let alone an actual sentence.

This issue isn't just limited to the computer communications generation. Even the presidents aren't exempt from initialisms. There's FDR, LBJ, and JFK. There's AA, not to be confused with Triple-A. There's the KKK who is watched by the CIA and/or the FBI, as are all of us by the IRS. There's TV, with channels like ABC, CBS, NBC, CNN, PBS, and TNT. I've always wondered if the SVU police drive in SUVs. You can have a reaction from MSG and be rushed to the ER where you can get CPR by an EMT or an RN and pray that it's covered by your HMO. This is the way things are in the USA, and special education is not exempt from it.

Special-ed is full of initialisms and acronyms that derive, of course, from the first letters of the words they stand for, in order. There should be courses taught at UCLA, BC, BU and NYU just for learning the over one hundred acronyms in special-ed. There are pages and pages of websites defining all of them. Just go to any "www" page that has to do with the subject. Every special-ed child in CT has an IEP (Individualized Educational Program) that was developed at a PPT (Planning and Placement Team) meeting. Once a child is identified, he or she is given a label. The label is always referred to by an acronym, like some sort of secret code. Some of these have stayed around, some have popped up more recently, and others have gone by the wayside as outdated or perhaps politically incorrect. Just to name a few, past and present, there are LD, PDD, OCD, ODD, OHI, EMR, EMH, MR, MD, DS, SS, ADD, and ADHD and ID (not to be confused with the ID you carry around with you, like the driver's license you need in case you get pulled over for a DWI).

Special education isn't alone in this though; education in general is loaded with initials. Just to name a few in CT, students are required to take the DRP (Degrees of Reading Power), DRA (Development Reading Assessment) and CMT (Connecticut Mastery Test). It all can just make you want to scream OMG!

Not the Natural Order of Things

The educational bureaucracy that goes along with the CMT and DRP/A tests makes me loathe these acronyms the most. I know I'm not being fair. I'm sure there is a logic behind the rules that I am not privy to. I'm sure it looks good and makes perfect sense somewhere beyond the classroom. Here's my point. Children who have gone through the PPT process and are labeled, say, as LD (Learning Disabled) each have an IEP. The teacher is supposed to follow the goals on the IEP and teach each child according to his or her level. The IEP takes time to plan and write up and consists of many pages. Included in it are the modifications that should be made for the child and notes on the child's strengths and weaknesses in various academic areas. There are the individual modifications, goals, and objectives for each of these areas and a mention of what grade level the child is performing on, along with how many hours per week the child will participate in the special program. So the BL (bottom line) is that the classroom and special education teacher get to work and present the material on the child's level.

When I was a resource room teacher, I had students who were in fifth grade whose IEPs stated they were reading on or about a mid-to-high third-grade level. I would follow the IEP according to law and teach them reading starting on or about that third-grade level. This seemed fair enough. Then came the CMTs and the DRP/A tests, which state that all students have to take the tests on their grade levels. What this means is a student in fifth grade who is being taught on a third-grade level, as the IEP mandates, has to take the test at a fifth-grade level. I hope you are still following me here. In fairness to the tests, they are in compliance with the modifications referred to on the IEP, such as test directions being read to them, the students are given more time, and so on. However, this does not change the fact that these children are sent in to take a test for a level at which they haven't been taught yet. Want to take a guess (even with modifications) how they are going to do?

It is almost as difficult to watch them struggle through these tests as it is for them to take it. If you were ever looking for the perfect opportunity to set a kid up for failure, look no further than to the acronyms CMT and DR. To add ITI (insult to injury…and yes, I made that one up), I was handed a paper to fill out after the testing was complete. On the paper was a list of my students who did not reach the expected outcome of the test. Next to each name were various blanks for me to fill in on such topics as: why I thought the child did not pass, what goals and objectives I could set to help the child, how much time should be put into that help. The answers were everything I had already written out on each child's planned program. I felt a rebellion coming on. It just wasn't natural to follow an order like this. Perhaps I could make a statement, short but to the point, of how ridiculous I thought this whole thing was. I reached out for an acronym to make my point. So across the paper that listed the names and asked for all the required information, I wrote "See IEP." So much for NCLB (No Child Left Behind)!

I did get some reprimands from the poor reading teacher and her supervisor, who were responsible for handing these in. They kept telling me I had to fill the papers out and I very politely said "I already did. It's all on the IEP." I didn't want to yell at them and shoot the messenger, but they were fairly persistent. I explained my reasons for not complying and told them I wanted to be called in by the state. I wanted to have to go to court. I wanted to be sued so I could sue them back for undue harsh treatment of my students and making me waste my time and taxpayers' money writing the same things over and over again. There were other reasons too. Like, why do they have a legal and binding IEP if no one is going to bother to look at it? No one from the state ever called me about it. There you go. The one time you beg to be sued and everyone ignores you. Don't you hate when that happens?

A New Order

Let me be perfectly clear. There are a lot of good, caring people out there in charge. I also admit that I would never want to have their jobs. I can't imagine what they must have to deal with. What I think would help would be to have everyone, absolutely everyone—

from the local to the federal people who create these laws and orders for teachers and schools to follow—substitute in different schools, in different systems and in different grades, for no less than two months. I don't mean observe. I mean teach, right down to the paperwork. If the response is that they don't have teaching degrees, then the question is, why are they in charge and why are they making the laws and orders? All in all, I think teaching could be more than just an enlightening experience for them, or a type of payback. They could combine their old knowledge, the parts that really work, with this new, hands-on wisdom and really move things ahead—or at the very least, possibly eliminate some of the chaos (which is a whole other theory we won't go into).

PART V
The Role Models

*

The models for modeling behavior

11
The Divine Interveners

What Made Me Think of Them

I had gotten into the habit of walking along the beach after school with one of the kindergarten teachers. It was good exercise and it gave us a chance to complain about the ridiculous amount of paperwork and the pressure we were under to cover an exorbitant amount of material in a ridiculously short amount of time. We were thinking maybe we should have gone to magic school, or at least taken a few courses in abra codabra. We kept walking and talking faster as our pace of depression increased with every word. When we were finally out of breath, we ended the conversation with the soulful lament, "After all the work, are we really teaching these kids anything? Are we making a difference?" Then, as if on some mystical cue, as we were passing two women standing together talking, one of them reached out to me and gave me a hug.

I would have hugged her back, but it was one of those unexpected encounters that leave one motionless. She moved back, hands still grasping my arms, said my name, looked at her friend, and said, "This is the woman God sent to me. This is the teacher who saved my son's life." I looked at her closely, studied her face, and remembered her. I had taught her son years ago. He had been on my caseload for most of grammar school. He was a great kid, a serious student, and she and her husband were parents who never lost faith in him and supported him with genuine care and concern. Still holding onto me, she told her friend about how I was the teacher who had taught him how to learn and told him he could definitely go on to college. Special education does not rule out higher education. He was now in college, doing well, and proud that his dreams were coming true.

I was speechless for a few moments. I mean, I *could* have run into the mother who had said to me "You're lucky I don't have my husband come beat the shit out of you." But I didn't. I ran into the mother who answered my question whether, at least in this case, I had taught something. It was a serendipitous divine intervention, so I smiled at her, gave her a hug and told her she was wrong. God had sent her to me, not me to her.

Not Making the Grade

I walked away so glad to know that I had helped this boy not to be left behind. I thought about the teachers who didn't leave *me* behind. In my wildest dreams I was never even close to an A student in grammar or most of high school. If they had had special-ed when I was in school, I would have been labeled learning disabled in auditory discrimination, memory, and figure-ground. Since there wasn't such a program, I spent part of my middle and high school career in the second-to-lowest sections.

I was told by my high school guidance counselor not to even bother applying to colleges because I would never get in. She suggested I set my sights on a job at a grocery store, probably the local one at the mall. Grocery store? I never shopped in a grocery store. I didn't even know how to cook. Raw meat made me squeamish. She knew nothing about me. She looked at some grades and stats written about me from nationwide tests on a piece of paper and made this ridiculous proclamation about my future. I mean, she could have had the courtesy to pick a record store or a bookstore, at least to fill my fantasy of being a musically inclined literary scholar. I stood to leave her office, grabbed a few of the college catalogs, signed them out, and left. Actions speak louder than words, and I couldn't repeat what I was thinking at the time. When I got early acceptance to the college of my choice, she was the first person I went to tell. Not that I hold a grudge.

Obviously, she wasn't one of my divine interveners. She wasn't one of the chalk-toting saints that didn't leave me behind. So who were they?

The Vast Enlightenment

There was a social studies teacher in middle school who was loud and excited. She taught with passion and the conviction that everything she was telling us was of the utmost importance. You could tell she loved it too, because almost everything she told us wasn't in the book, it was in her head. She knew her stuff cold and she made me want to know it all too. She would entice us with little spicy stories that the sterilized book never even mentioned. She let us know that our heroes were human and flawed, which, of course, made them much more fascinating. She filled us in on the real plight of the Native American, way past some turkey-and-corn feast in November. Did she teach me names and dates and places? I don't really remember and I don't really care. She did teach me to love to learn on my own. She taught me to love research, to be involved with what I was studying. She taught to me care about what I was learning. She taught me how to take learning outside the classroom and how to leave the textbook in the classroom. She taught us we can make a difference. I wasn't being left behind in the classroom, I was moving ahead in life armed with interest and passion.

Making History

My high school history teacher was very different from the middle school social studies teacher. He was a quiet man, subdued in everything, including his wardrobe. He had that friendly but distant manner. He was like a tranquilizer. He wasn't boring, he just didn't express excitement. The class listened and liked him in a friendly but distant way. I probably would have passed him by as one of my divine interveners if it wasn't for the fact that he picked me for a very special event.

He kept me after class one day to tell me that Yale University was running a program. History teachers in local towns were to choose a student to be part of an event. On Saturdays, these chosen students would meet at Yale to be presented with various lectures and then meet with a graduate student to discuss the lecture topic. He chose me to be that student. I was floored. I knew I wasn't the best student in the class, so I asked him why he had picked me. He said that I didn't have the highest grade in the class, but I was a good thinker and asked well-thought-out questions, and that made me the person who he felt would get the most from the program. I could have kissed this hero of a man who on any other occasion would just have blended into the woodwork.

I was going to Yale, not to the grocery store! This would be my only chance to go to Yale, because for one thing I would never get in, and for another, Yale didn't accept women when I was in high school. It was great, and it is amazing how when you don't have to take notes, when there's no pressure to get good grades and memorize material, you have more time to sit and really think about what is being said. I remember sitting in one of the huge, Oxfordesque halls, usually reserved for male students only, listening to Rev. William Sloane Coffin. I remember he said something that was really worth thinking about and something that stayed with me my whole life. The first part went something like, "Do not fear the person that loves you, for all he can do is hurt you. Do not fear the person who hates you, for all he can do is kill you." (Ouch.) The last part I remember perfectly: "But fear the person who is apathetic, for he can destroy you."

My placid-appearing history teacher saw me as a person with potential, not just some student in his room with an average grade. He pushed me ahead to hear a comment that would become the basis for how I looked at many things in life, and specifically teaching. Strange how some people come into your life. I can't say that I remember anything specific that he taught me, so in that sense he shouldn't stand out as a great teacher. He wasn't the one who said the quote that became so profound to me, so in that sense he shouldn't stand out either. It's not what he was, it's what he *wasn't* that made him a divine intervener. He wasn't apathetic. He was interested and involved enough to see what I would care about and he allowed me that opportunity and I learned from it. I learned to see that apathy does destroy, but any experienced teacher and politician could tell you that. You can't move someone who doesn't care. There is no action or reaction from indifference. You can't defeat ignorance with an army of students who don't care about the battle.

It's All Greek to Me

Math was never my best subject, but I got by as long as just numbers were involved. It was when they started throwing in letters and phrases like "*y* to the fifth power" that I really became completely baffled. Letters are symbols that make sounds, so what does 4x + 2y + 3xy + 5 say? There were other questions. Did a capital letter have more "power" than a lowercase letter? My mind just couldn't make the transition or the translation. I mean, you can add all the *x*'s and *y*'s you want, but they don't say a thing without a vowel. I was plagued with confusing nomenclature in the language of algebra, whose variables just left me with a few expressions of my own I'd rather not repeat.

Luckily, my first algebra teacher was a woman of honor. I still got a D, but she never let me feel insecure about it. I tried because I liked her and no matter how stupid my answer was to one of her questions, she never rolled her eyes, put her hands on her hips, or made a humiliating comment. Instead, she looked like she was giving my answer some thought, looked at the board, looked at me, and said something like, "I can see why you would think that," or "That's an interesting answer…very interesting." Or "Good answer. It isn't right, but it's a good answer." She said it with such sincerity that no one laughed or thought of snickering.

When she walked around and came to where I was sitting, she would take her time and go over the examples with me like I was on the right track, even though I had never even caught the math train. Didn't she leave me behind at the station? No, she took me as far as I could go. What she gave me was the highest respect and amazement for something I will never understand. I didn't hate algebra; I was in awe of it. Math became spiritual to me—something you don't really understand but have great faith in all its powers just the same, even *y* to its highest power.

More Greek

Along with math, I have a deep and abiding respect for chemistry. This is due to the same inability I had to grasp it and to an amazing teacher who taught it in college. If it hadn't been required I never would have taken it. I signed up for a summer course so I would have more time to focus on my failure. I sat in the front row, raised my hand to ask questions, and went to the professor after class for help. He spent a lot of time with me, gave me easier high school books to use and even assigned me my own, free, private grad student tutor.

I was going into the final with a D. The professor wished me luck and smiled as I sat down to the final test. I flunked it. When my grade was mailed to me I was shocked. I had a C. I had pangs of guilt that someone out there was mistakenly walking around with my F, so I made an appointment to see the professor and let him know of this error. I figured I'd get caught in the long run because no self-respecting C student would take my F lying down.

The professor told me it wasn't a mistake at all. He had given me the C. He actually went so far as to change my less-than-45 average to a 75. As bad as I was in math, I knew enough to know that this was an unheard-of leap to a thirty-point raise. He had me sit down as he explained that he was actually flattered at how hard I had tried and that it was also obvious that I would never pass chemistry. He said there was no point in making me repeat the course and no point in failing me, which would prevent me from getting my teaching degree. He did ask that I never teach chemistry. I gave my Scout's honor that I wouldn't…and didn't break that promise for thirty-two years.

I got up from my seat. I thanked him from all levels of my heart and I told him with great passion, my index finger pointing in his direction, that I may have flunked his course, but he was the best teacher I ever had. I may have been left behind in chemistry but I learned that common sense, compassion, and a lack of professional ego are so important to teaching. They also were much more usable and important skills in my life than the periodic table. That's not to say that chemistry, biology, physics, and all the rest aren't important. They are vital, amazing, and a bit beyond my realm of thinking. But I wouldn't trade what I learned in his class for all the scientific discourse analysis in the world.

12

The Saving Graces

We all cringe at the recollection of those students who have stretched our patience to the end of our fraying rope, and made us feel like every day, even at age thirty, was a midlife crisis. Not to mention those who had us seriously consider that overindulging in alcohol consumption should be part of our health care program. I don't want to think about these kids. Why should I let them crowd my brain and leave no room for the saving-grace students? (The word "grace" has multiple meanings. I'll let you look them up, though you probably don't have to.) These students are the ones who gently reach out and send us a life raft while we're floundering in the murky waters, wondering why we became teachers.

They are, no matter what their intelligence, great students. They may or may not be the most popular, most athletic, tallest, shortest, musically inclined, artistically outstanding, or best dressed. They aren't consumed with drawing attention to themselves, nor are they particularly shy. They seldom fall prey to other kids picking on them for the mere fact that they can hold their own under almost any circumstance and chalk the insult up to someone being obtuse. They are kind, secure, focused, and filled with goodwill. They ooze common sense. They are born with wisdom and maturity—sometimes a bit more maturity than we have ourselves.

The Fire Drill

There are three types of fire drills at schools. The first is where everyone in the school knows when that bell is going to ring. Teachers have agenda book in hand (now it's a laptop or ipad) and all students are sitting at their desks with a "ready, set, go" demeanor. The second type is when just the staff knows when, and they hover over the class, constantly watching the clock. The timing of the third type is only known to the administrators, which can cause some pretty embarrassing and chaotic events to ensue.

On one spring day, the third type of alarm was sounded. I left the building and took my assigned position by one of the side doors to monitor the classes leaving. A friend of mine and her third-grade class approached me as they came marching out. I was caught completely off guard by the hysterical laughter. Kids bumping into each other and even hiccupping could be heard while some tried to catch their breath between sobs of merriment. Only two people weren't laughing: the classroom teacher and one of my saving graces, who stood right behind her.

The teacher looked at me and posed in a ridged stance of anger and astonishment. "Do you believe this class?" she asked me. I had no response, being as bewildered as she. It was when she turned to face her motley crew to yell a variety of grade-appropriate condemnations that I understood what was going on with them. With all her berating, they still conducted themselves like a group of miniature drunken sailors. Everything became perfectly clear and I, too, burst out laughing.

It seems that when the fire drill type-three bell rang, she had been in the middle of a hasty trip to the bathroom. In her rush to get to her class, she neglected to do the necessary final check and didn't notice that she had tucked the back of her skirt into the waistband of her panty hose. This was one of those situations where toilet paper stuck on the bottom of a shoe would have been a blessing.

As a colleague and friend, I would have told her why the class was laughing when she turned around to look at me once more. I just couldn't. Not because I didn't want to, but because *I* couldn't stop laughing. That was when the saving grace stepped in and took over. *"Oh, for God's sake!"* I heard her call as she grabbed the back of the teacher's waistband and yanked out the skirt. I should have done that. She was at that moment much more adult than I was. And when I think back on that day, I can't help it. I still crack up laughing.

I'm going to stop now, though I could go on. I'd rather sit back and call to mind more of the graces. Maybe you should, too. Indulge yourself for a moment, not in alcoholic beverages, but in thinking about those students who supported you when you were stumbling through the day or felt like you were talking to the wall. When you made a clever pun or joke and stared out at a sea of blank faces but found that one who was smiling back at you. These graces are the stuff that teaching is made of. They teach us as well as we teach them. They are the students who make you feel like you have less of a feeling of authority and more of a sense of purpose. They are the ones who should court our memories.

To my saving graces, I offer thanks for the memories, the maturity, and the saving of my sanity. I hope to be just like you when I grow up.

SECTION 2

STRATEGIES

PART VI
Departing from the Text

*

Discretion may be the better part of valor, but fervor is the greater part of teaching. All's fair in love and learning (with some discretion, of course).

13

Teaching What You Love

It's All About Me
(That's why it's such a short chapter)

If you're in a rush, this is probably a section you can skip. There is nothing here to do with required academics or even anything you would find useful as topic material. You may even find it a tad depressing, reminding you of something that has sat on your wish list since the day you thought of becoming a teacher. It's about teaching for the love of it while teaching what you love.

I should warn you that this chapter is embarrassingly narcissistic. I get a bit carried away on the subject of things that I'm impassioned about. It becomes all about me. Which, if you think about it, would be good for a teacher—if every once in a while you could stand in front of that class unworried about grades, scores, or a deadline … just stand there teaching, smiling, and all engrossed in what you were saying while watching a sea of little faces, wide eyed and anticipating your every word. You might expound on places you've traveled to, astronomy, magic tricks, the *Titanic*…anything from the tasty traits of your favorite recipe to the subject of the Red Sox versus the Yankees. With this passion comes a way to work what you love to learn about into what makes them love to learn with all those required academic skills snuck in.

There was a time when you could sneak a few moments of these scholarly delusions of grandeur into the day. A time when every minute of the day didn't have to be weighed, measured, and documented. A time when you could teach not only the dictated, mandated curriculum with its correlating handouts and workbook pages, but go the extra mile on the road less traveled and depart from the text. There was a time when you could actually teach to kids instead of teaching to the test. A time when you could cast the reading, math, social studies and science book into time-out and try that novel idea: teaching students how to stretch their minds. Oh, those were the days. Now, they just about have enough room in the day to stretch their legs, and the only thing expanding is not their thirst for knowledge but their waistlines. It was a healthier way to teach, on many levels.

Teach I did. I taught (mostly fifth graders and some others too) Shakespeare, Mediaeval English history, and what I call "environmental circle thinking" using Native American culture. I picked these because I'm an avid quoter of the Bard, a fanatical mediaeval Anglophile, and a tree-hugging environmentalist. I was brilliant (there's that narcissistic boasting thing I was talking about). But actually, who really cares? The real point is, the *students* were brilliant, and they knew it. They were proud of it. They were so impressive that I decided to rebel, to overlook the times and still teach these subjects even when it became taboo to do so. Whoever would have thought that Shakespeare, English kings, and the environment would be excluded from academics? Go figure.

Once I was exhausted from patting myself on the back, I started to really think this issue out as it affected my students more than how it affected me. Maybe, just maybe, these kids weren't so much learning disabled as we were forced into being "teaching disabled." Teach children that they can learn, in the way that they learn, and feed their curiosity and you are more than halfway there. If I pick a topic or vehicle that I love and use it to teach and reinforce skills, then I can be extremely motivated, passionate, and spontaneous. If I am that way, I can pass that on to the students. I mean, how excited can you really be about teaching the six syllable types, prepositional phrases, and expository writing without a little exterior stimulus—or at least some disguise and dress-up? What I found so impressive, too, was how it made the kids feel. Even their posture seemed to improve along with their enthusiasm. They wanted to learn. They wanted to do a great job. They knew they could succeed.

The small secret to this success was not me or even what I was teaching. Hard to admit. It was the fact that these kids were learning things that were taught in high school. Okay, the method and length of time spent on the subject were not high-school level, but that didn't seem to matter. Most important, because they were learning something no one else was being taught, there was no way to measure their success. They couldn't compare how they were doing against everyone else, because no one else was doing it. They were the best and the pressure was off, and most, most important, they knew they could learn. They felt smart, and they were.

It only got better for my resource room students when I took the subjects to their regular fifth grade classes. I could do this thanks to the wonderful teachers I worked with. I would always prep my own students before teaching in the class, so they already knew some of the answers and looked brilliant. If that's cheating, then I don't care. Once I taught one of these topics to the entire fifth grades, you could see the change of attitude in the special-ed students—*and* the rest of the class when I went to take them from the room. Their stigma changed to status. Some non-special-ed students even wanted to go with them, so every once in a while they were allowed to bring a guest.

One fifth-grade student summed it all up. It was parent-teacher conference night. This boy and his mom were sitting outside his classroom waiting their turn when I walked by. He and I exchanged greetings as I passed. I heard the mother ask him who I was. He responded, "She's the special teacher."

The mother asked, "Special education?"

"No," he said, looking at her as if she had just grown two heads. "She teaches special things."

Special education just got redefined. It went back to being a good thing.

14
Mediaeval History

Have you ever wondered what draws you like a magnet to certain things? It's like love at first sight, some type of awe-inspiring chemistry, some long-lost friend, or a part of yourself that you suddenly rediscover. You could say it's something imprinted in your DNA or genes going back mega-generations, possibly reincarnation, or just some cosmic, quirky, happenstance moment. Whatever the cause, there you are, completely enthralled with some aspect of the natural or manufactured world that others may find completely mundane. When someone's trash is someone else's treasure, there's no accounting for taste or room for judgment calls.

Who's Buried Where

One of my eccentric enthusiasms that verges on neurotic obsession is the lives of long-dead British nobility. Perhaps more aptly put, I'm a mediaeval Anglophile. In my case, I chalk it up to some past-life, kindred-spirit thing, because I, by nature, spell like Chaucer and have that mediaeval love/hate relationship with grammar and punctuation. The rather lonely, isolating fact about any such interest is if you are not around others who share your passion, you have the problem of what to do with all that knowledge. I decided to solve this dilemma by teaching what I knew to my fifth-grade inclusion students, just for the fun of it.

It was really a no-brainer. Between my exuberance and the meaty, juicy stories I was telling, they were sucked in right from the beginning. I brought in my extensive collection of photos of tombs of English kings and queens, which I traveled through England and France to take (I usually don't admit that to too many people). I also brought a substantial number of mature history books, including my favorite about who's buried where in England.

The kids and I went to town writing our own little history book. I even snuck in various academic skills without them actually noticing, or at least not seeming to. I really started to believe that old cooking proverb: "It's all in the presentation." We made lists on the board of "good" words to use. If there was a word they didn't know in one of the books they were reading, we took it apart in syllables. There was no embarrassment about not knowing a word. They didn't mind asking for help because they were told ahead of time that these were college books. It was okay, because truth be told, in this one situation they weren't catching up with kids in the regular classes, they were moving ahead of them.

Each student chose a favorite historical character that I had probably talked ad nauseam about during my introduction, always including some obscure details that added a personal touch about each person. Sometimes I wondered if the kids chose certain people because they felt some connection to them. Whatever the reason, they were engrossed in independent study. Sitting at the table, they meandered through the books and photographs, taking notes and sharing what they found with each other. I ran around the group, explaining various aspects of the person that would be difficult for them to grasp directly from the material. It was perfect. As I helped sound out, spell, or define words, the students were partaking in a random and spontaneous reinforcement of reading, spelling, writing, and comprehension skills. We worked on complete sentences, verb tenses, and extending their vocabulary with more word choices.

Not wanting to exclude math, we borrowed, carried, multiplied, and divided our way through dates to find out how old someone was, or how old he or she would be now, or even transposing the value of mediaeval money into ours. They really liked this project, since they enhanced their stories by using all those boring skills whose purpose now made sense. I watched them transform themselves from students into scholars. They even listened to a tape of a person reading the introduction of *The Canterbury Tales* in the original Middle English. It's amazing what they'll find noteworthy when the pressure is off and good, old-fashioned curiosity gets a little breathing room.

Jeopardy

One girl caught me outside one morning on my way into school. She was breathless with excitement as she told me she had been watching *Jeopardy* with her parents the night before. The information asked for on the show was the name of the father of King Henry IV of England. She had quickly blurted out, "John of Gaunt." The TV verified that she was absolutely correct, which absolutely shocked her parents. "They didn't even know that!" She beamed as she added, "They thought I was so smart."

"Feels great, doesn't it?" I asked. She agreed, but didn't have to. You could see it in her smile, in her posture, and entire demeanor that she believed she was now admired, respected, smart, and most important, studious. This new feeling of smart and studious made almost anything possible. She walked into school ready to seize the day. John of Gaunt may have had little to do with any test question or life skill, but he opened up a whole new world for her. I love when that happens.

History vs. Social Studies

I had a prize student once in my unit on kings and queens of Old England. I would have picked him as a future candidate for that special course at Yale. So you can imagine my shock when he showed me his report card: he had a D in social studies. I questioned him on how this could possibly be. He raised his hand, pointing to the classroom and declared, "*That* is social studies." He then pointed to our worktable and confirmed, "*This* is history." Well, that gave me a lot to ponder. How come he couldn't see the history in social studies? How could he so easily separate them from each other? Worst of all, how could he not be interested in the history that was taught in social studies?

After much brainstorming and deliberation, I concluded that his social studies class must have been taught with a focus on a historical timeline, not a sociological one, and I thought that was unfortunate. After all, if society is under discussion, then it is good to note what makes that society the way it is. That means that time periods that don't necessarily impact the particular area you are concentrating on can be skipped. You can jump around, all over history, to make the proper connections. Ergo, although chronological order is important, sticking to it strictly can completely obscure cause and effect. (Remember, this is social studies, not earth science.) Not to mention, it has never proven to inspire interest in the subject matter being chronicled whatsoever. It doesn't give the students anything to sink their teeth into or show them why the subject should be memorable. This is when I concluded that the only thing left to do was to take my Middle Ages enthusiasm into the regular classroom. I mean, I needed a perfect excuse to continue pontificating on my passions, and this was as close to perfect as I was going to get.

Jolly Old England and Our Civil War

I decided, in the spirit of social studies and not history, and to fulfill my grand design to share my knowledge with as many students as possible, that the classes that were studying the Civil War were the best places to teach my unit on "historic" kings and dead citizens of England. The Civil War's prevalent causes—slavery, the opposing mores of the north and south, and the contest between revered freedoms and financial gluttony that fed the fire of civil unrest—all led back across the pond to Britain. I do make the very important point somewhere in my sharing that we are not to form harsh judgments or play holier-than-thou against these predecessors of our nation. In their circumstances, we really don't know what we would have done. I also mentioned that some of the events and people that were being left out would emphatically contradict some of the points we were generally making. This was an overview presentation; plus, time was of the essence and I couldn't cover everything. These "blanks" actually motivated a few, rare students to dig even deeper. They love to prove you wrong.

Usually, most students feel a bit thrown off jumping from 1800s USA to the idea of twelfth-century England as the backdrop for slavery, but they are inquisitive, and that seems to keep their attention. I begin with King John and march up through time to Elizabeth I. I like to begin with the worst king. Villains seem to quiet the masses. I also introduce the signing of the Magna Carta and its importance to our form of government. The eyebrows do raise a bit when the class hears that John was so awful a king and human being that it is believed that monks killed him by poisoning his favorite fruit: peaches. After he died and all of England celebrated, the people declared, "We'll have no king named John!" (And to this day, they never *have* had another king named John.) We jump up to the Plantagenets and how they got their name. Things like the harsh treatment of serfs, the practice of "hang, draw, and quarter," and the lack of personal hygiene are always attention grabbers.

The section on Edward III to Henry VIII is accompanied with a family tree across the board. Lines are drawn to, and *x*'s placed by, each king that was killed by a cousin. I have Richard III calling out "A horse, a horse, my kingdom for a horse!" Those two young princes buried in the wall of London Tower and all of Henry's VIII's wives' names and history are given, including the causes of their demise, be it in divorce or just off with their heads. Bloody Mary reminds them of Halloween and is probably the all-time favorite. By the time we reach Elizabeth, their little heads are spinning, I'm completely out of breath, and the board looks like the wreck of the Hesperus. One student inevitably asks, "How do you know all this?"

I always give the same two-word answer: "I read." I also tell them that their books leave pretty much all the good stuff out, so either go to the library or try the web.

The Tie-In

So what does this have to do with slavery and the Civil War? Glad you asked. It gives students a new vested interest in the War and in their personal histories. Here are some of the points in my argument. First of all, if the history of England had been different—say, King John was a nice guy and the Magna Carta was never signed—then our country's history and relationship to democracy might have been different, or perhaps, it might never have been founded at all.. It might have meant that many of us would never have been born, because our parents or grandparents and so on back would never have come to this country to meet.

Second, the king, along with his kin, was considered deemed by God and country at birth to be better than other people. "Is this true?" I ask the class. I lead them in a huge "*No!*" just in case someone might consider the possibility. I ask them to imagine that the classroom is a town in Old England. I tell them we are all serfs and go into detail about that life. So we really have no rights. We are told what to do and even what to think. We have to be the same religion as the king and our noble leader or else we are killed by burning at the stake, or the old hang, draw and quarter, or off with your head. I get pretty lengthy on how they were banned from any education pertaining to the skills of reading, writing and arithmetic. To the king their ignorance was his bliss. Now, here comes the rub.

For the most part, relatives of the rich and noble people were the ones who moved down to the American south and started plantations. They had slaves because they were used to having cheap labor from the serfs. Slavery was okay by them, because they were better than others by the mere fact that they were born that way, or so they liked to think. Nice work if you can get it. On the other hand, the people who wanted a different religion than the king's, those who really could claim "religious persecution," were the people who escaped England (mostly by way of Holland) and moved up to the American north. They could relate to people who wanted freedoms and had a touch of understanding of what the slaves had to go through.

There are complicating factors, like the cotton gin and other political issues, and the fact that there was slavery up north as well—including that of some Native Americans—but the students see them against a background now. They are connected. It starts to make sense, and with that comes a level of interest. Our books tend to be focused on the cut and dried—and all those dates! I like to take a few poetic liberties by adding personal touches to the historical cast of characters. Things like, "Do you think Richard II was scared or nervous when he became king at eleven years old? Do you think that's what made him such a lousy, neurotic, paranoid, and jealous king?" Personalizing historical people and giving a touch of some unknown facts, or commonly heard historical quotes flying through the classroom from your lips to their ears, go a long way toward humanizing the people they are reading about.

Did you know that Richard II invented the handkerchief? Too bad the kids don't know what those are anymore.

How Sweet the Sound

Perhaps the fairy-tale nuances and slight historical embellishments aren't for you. Maybe music is more your style. I love music myself. So, let me suggest another Englishman, who was not a king but was much more directly connected with the time and location of the Civil War: John Newton, writer of "Amazing Grace," a song closely associated with the war and slavery. Here's a great story of a wretched man who was in fact a slave trader. A huge, vicious storm hit the ship he was on. It changed his life and inspired him to write the words that later became the song. There he saw his own possible death coming as he witnessed the lightning, high winds, and waves in the darkness, and the sound of the thunder in the sky. He was petrified. He had at that moment what is called an epiphany. There's poetry, music, metaphor, history, and tons of angst in this story. It's a great introduction to the subject of slavery and the war. It's also great for prompting some to reflect on their own short-sighted actions. Even kids have things to feel wretched about.

The Race for Good Relations

If the class is mature enough or if it's an older group, the study of how the Civil War was connected with the social mores of Old England and even John Newton could be a good time to introduce the relationships between races and how many wars have been started based on social ego and ignorance. I mean all the issues, fights, wars and prejudice over color, when basically, it all comes down to the need for vitamin D. Many mouths drop, many eyes pop open when you tell the vitamin D story of life. It's also a good way to promote some interest in the study of science.

There are also some positive social aspects of these wars for students to ponder. For one, the Civil War appears to be one of the first occasions when there were people of one race who went against others of their own to defend people of another race, all for the sake of justice. A good example to give is the one about the lawyer Theodore Sedgwick in Massachusetts, who freed Elizabeth Freeman and a man named Brom, using the United States's new Constitution to do it. Sedgwick showed that a man could fight for the rights of another race and that it could be done in court by a jury of *Sedgwick's* peers, not Elizabeth's, with a peaceful and legal resolution. Now, there's a lesson in history about social graces, not to mention political correctness! Food for thought, discussion, and independent research abounds in this study of social behavior and, dare I say it, history.

The Meat Wagon

I would be ecstatic to pontificate on the "Lady of Shalott" lesson. Luckily, you are off the hook. I could talk a dog off a meat wagon when it comes to this, and I know it. Just think, though, about where your own dog and meat wagon lie and share it. Tie it in. You're still teaching, and don't let anyone tell you you're not. No one said that you can't get creative when teaching. If they did say that, then just ignore them or explain that you once were lost, but now you're found, and it all happened during this huge storm while you were out at sea. That should, if nothing else, get them to leave you alone.

15
Shakespeare

Just Another Good Ol' Boy

If you follow the motto "can't get enough of a good thing" (or a good obsession), then you will understand how I traveled from mediaeval England to Renaissance England. I did make a leap and dropped the kings and queens for the famous writer Shakespeare. It wasn't a huge leap, since he wrote so many plays about mediaeval kings. I contemplated the pros and cons of taking him with me to the fifth grade. I had to conquer the ever-prevailing notion passed down through the centuries that fifth graders were, by sheer age, cognitive development, and lack of life experiences, too young for the Bard. I had some issues with this.

The greatest hurdle to jump was the misconception about his snob appeal. Just because *we* associate snobbery with Shakespeare, it by no means indicates that he himself was a snob. Au contraire. He was a man of the masses and appealed to the common and bawdy, to vigorous applause. Considering that common and bawdy are the most popular values in today's entertainment, I figured Shakespeare was a shoo-in.

The next biggest argument against taking the Bard to the fifth was the difficulty of the language. Oh, please! Have you ever listened to the way these kids speak? Shakespeare's English is a breeze for them. Then there's the content area—it's way too complex for them to grasp with their little minds. Another *Oh, please!* Shakespeare's plays are classics, remember? They are called that for a reason. Apart from the incest innuendoes and wife killing, which should be saved for later years, they are filled with sword fights, battles, betrayal, heroes, villains, troll-like mortals, and tons of paternal and maternal angst. It's every fifth grader's plotline dream.

Nothing to Fear but Fear Itself

Let's face it. Be honest. Adults are afraid of Shakespeare. We sat through those high school and college classes bored silly. If we were lucky, we became mesmerized by iambic pentameter and it lulled our brains to sleep. The problem is, we should have been introduced to Shakespeare in fifth grade. Kids that age don't know yet that Shakespeare is a boring snob who speaks weird English and writes about nothing of interest. It's a time before indoctrination when *Hamlet*, *Henry V*, and a choice of a comedy can seem like old friends instead of decrepit, alien creatures.

Now that the argument for depriving fifth graders of the most excellent Will seemed to me like *Much Ado aAbout Nothing*, I plotted my approach. I tweaked the so-called language barrier, plucked out the inappropriate, shrunk the meanings to child size, enhanced it all with background and with a dab of this and a dollop of that. Shakespeare was prepared to be served up and devoured by a ravenous audience, hungry for a meal they had never tasted:

the old-world classics. It's like spinach. Dress it up enough, give it some avant-garde, "wow"-enhancing PR, and they'll think they're eating the best processed, chemically enhanced, plastic-wrapped junk food.

The Passport

All jesting aside, I had a good feeling about Shakespeare's success. I had some practice with the English kings lessons and there was this subtle "something" that I finally was able to put my finger on: I realized that I wasn't "teaching" them anything. I was taking them somewhere. We were traveling together and I was the tour guide.

There is, I surmised, a huge difference between lecturing, teaching, and sharing. They all have to do with imparting knowledge of some kind. We lecture and we teach, but how often do we get to share? I was going in equipped with my desire to share the joy of Shakespeare. The positions of the students change when you share. They move from their desks and chairs as subordinates to a location of equality. You are giving them something that you hope will make them happy and excited. It comes through in your voice, your mannerisms, in the way you answer their questions and respond to their comments. It's subtle, but not by any means unimportant, nor does it go unnoticed. I've noticed other teachers do it. I've sat in classrooms, my mental passport ready to depart, thrilled to be included on their voyage to a novel location filled with insight.

I began my journey to "Shakespeare's England" with basic background about his life and times. Behind me were visual aids: a *Henry V* movie poster complete with a sword and a battle scene and a poster with a portrait of Will sporting long hair and an earring — good attention getters. The itinerary includes telling the kids how much I hated Shakespeare in high school and my suggestion that when they take those classes, they cheat (within academic reason, of course) and use a study guide in book form or off the web.

I can say that because it's true. We missed the boat on that one. The reason is so obvious: Shakespeare wrote three things. He wrote poems and sonnets and plays. Plays are made to be seen, not read. If he had wanted us to read them, he would have written books. It's awful, it's painful, to sit there and read about all these strange people with strange names speaking a strange language in some strange place. We are doing Old Will a grave injustice and probably would have him spinning in his grave if he had one (he's in a tomb in his local church). So I tell the students that when in high school, yes, cheat—and if there's a movie, watch it and *then* read the play. Boy, am I popular!

Then came the language issue. I presented it as a challenge. I enlightened the students about why Shakespeare is taught in high school: because most adults think that fifth graders are too young and not smart enough yet to understand him or his vernacular. I told them that I know this "fact" is a fallacy, and that they could prove all these adults wrong by showing that they were actually better at deciphering Shakespeare's English than the grown-ups. They were ready to defy the masses, embrace the idea of cheating, and move ahead.

For our excursion, I am the cheat-sheet study guide. I do all the cheating for them. I give them the background of the story. I define the poet's English and write the names of the characters on the board, usually in syllables, and then the phonic way to pronounce them. I use keywords that stress personalities and emotions. I'm filled with them, so it just flows, sometimes one right into the other.

We watch the pertinent and appropriate parts of a movie, and I stop at certain points. I tell them what's going to happen. I quote speeches and explain what they mean. I ask questions that I myself might have asked after seeing the clip. I become Shakespeare's chorus, and I'm brimming with "a muse of fire." Either the kids are extremely polite, feeling sorry for me for being so weird, or they truly get caught up in the expedition, because the room is jam-packed with a longing for what is to come.

Hamlet

The first place I take them to is Denmark. *Hamlet* is the play where brother kills brother for power and a wife, where ghosts appear ruefully ranting for vengeance, and where every person but one meets with some grisly death by the end. Now, there's a cheery fellowship of losers. I can see in my mind academia shaking its brilliant heads and pooh-poohing this endeavor. What academics fail to see, though, is that classics, like wedding cakes and winter wardrobes, have layers. Layers are wonderful things. They circumvent all the customary restrictions, boundaries, preconceived notions, and curriculum-based requirements. They leave you free, with no need to impress anyone or worry about condemnation. Free to scrutinize each layer of the particular classic and pick and choose what you want to focus on and how generously you want to indulge other layers. Shakespeare is a movable feast.

We dabble with "To be or not to be…" and the other heady speeches and concepts. Our focus, though, was on "To thine own self be true, And it must follow, as the night the day, Thou canst not then be false to any man." These wise and prophetic words were stated by Polonius, a foolish and meddlesome man. There alone is a bit of Shakespearean irony. It also leads to a good class discussion about why we should "practice what we preach." For Polonius it was too late; his busybody attitude got him killed and sent to sea, where Hamlet tells the king he is at supper—"Not where he eats, but where he is eaten." This is what happens when we don't listen to our own good advice.

Friendship

We tested the advice of this quote as it relates to friendship, looking at the type of friends the students wanted to have and the type of friends they wanted to be. We watched each character to see if they were true or not to themselves or others. As they meet with a death "most foul, strange, and unnatural," it becomes clear the advice was not taken. Friendship is the vehicle for *Hamlet*. They get it. Fifth graders are social animals and friendship is imperative to communal survival. Shakespeare makes this point so clearly in the story and gives some obviously powerful examples.

Rosencrantz and Guildenstern are neither the friends you want to have nor the friend you want to be. When it's off with your head, payback's a bitch. Horatio, on the other hand, is the hero of the story, the supreme role model for friendship and being true to oneself. He is also the only one still alive at the end of the play and sends his friend Hamlet to the next life with "Good night, sweet prince may flights of angels sing thee to thy rest."

We meander through the basic gloom, doom, despair, and despondency of the story. The kids amaze me with how much of what is going on soaks in. One remedial reading student stated at the end, "Wow, this is all about betrayal." We discussed the meaning of "betrayal." Obviously, he got it and I doubt will soon forget it. One girl made the observation that although both Claudius and Laertes plotted murder and carried it through, they were both wrong but not both evil. When asked why she thought this, she stated that it was because Claudius's reason was greed and power while Laertes felt hurt and grief. Out of the mouths of babes.

Is all this a bit on the dark side for fifth graders? You wouldn't think so if you ever saw the computer games they play. The antiquity of the Shakespearean setting helps to distance a lot of the disconcerting action from them. How they do respond is with a curious respect. They take Shakespeare and what he has to say seriously. The man has a message for them, and they are listening. Best of all, they are thinking. They are left feeling important and empowered. Old Will wasn't kidding when he said "The play's the thing!"

The Play's the Thing...Along with the Movie

One class that had an amazing "renaissance teacher" requested to do a performance of *Hamlet*. We were both thrilled—and luckily it was long enough ago that we could actually squeeze it into the days ahead.

I touched up and shortened the story. We videotaped the performance so we could do one scene at a time. In complete contrast with and rebellion from the Elizabethan era, where boys played the women's parts, we let the girls play the men's parts. We even had more than one person play each character. The costumes, which a wonderfully talented designer friend made, were the keys to the characters. One girl died so well as Polonius that we let her play most of the death scenes. We weren't going for academy awards.

Our reward was standing behind the class as they requested, watching them watch the movie *Hamlet* in its entirety. They were spellbound. I almost wondered if they were going into that iambic-pentameter-memorizing trance. Then came the part where Hamlet pokes fun at Polonius and his stupidity in the library, and they started to laugh. They were *supposed* to laugh. They not only got the language, they got the jokes. They may have been laughing, but their teacher and I could have cried with pride. They left the land of sophomoric and entered the realm of sophisticated Shakespeareans. Could there possibly be anything left for us to teach?

Henry V

Yes, there was. There was *Henry V*— my personal favorite and one step up from *Hamlet*—because it offered the one important thing that *Hamlet* missed: redemption. Everyone loves an offer of redemption, and I just love *Henry V*. It was a win-win. I prefaced the play with a peek into Henry's younger days. He was a wild and crazy kid. Off at Oxford College, he never studied, partied all the time, drank, and hung around with a bad bunch of hooligans. He never got in trouble for anything he did because he was a prince, and they were pretty much exempt from any laws. (If nothing else, this fact promotes a greater interest in the government of monarchies.) The catalyst for all this bad behavior was his uncle, the king, who basically held him hostage. Old Uncle Richard II cleverly managed to manipulate Henry against his own father due to an abundance of political intrigue and family dissension and jealousies. It's the tangled web syndrome, and Henry is caught in the middle. Cutting through the chase of kings, Henry gets his turn at the throne.

"Oh, for a Muse of Fire"

This is the opening of the play, where the Chorus begs us to imagine the stage for a kingdom and a "Warlike Harry, like himself, Assume the port of Mars," in the vast and mighty fields of Agincourt where he will defeat the French. And he *is* like the god Mars, for a miraculous thing happens. This boy, of whom the bishop said he "never noted in him any study," does a complete turnaround, taking life and his responsibilities seriously—and he is on his way to becoming a great, good, and noble king. There's the rub; unlike Hamlet, he is redeemed. There is hope—and kids, like adults, love the idea of hope.

I think our first problem in teaching history is that we never tell about the great leaders' faults or transgressions. We always make them sound so perfect that kids can't relate to them. Take the old cherry tree story about George Washington. By the time they're ten, they've told enough lies to kill any chance of being like young George; ergo, they are not the stuff that great people are made of. So George and all the other names on the hero list seem vague and removed from themselves. Henry, on the other hand, showed real promise for the promise of redemption. Students could relate to him. He was their hero.

I gained a bit of respect from the boys with my detailed knowledge of the legendary battle. Most learn verbatim the "St. Crispin Day" speech, also known for the famous phrase "band of brothers." Or perhaps their respect is for my overzealous recitation of the speech. Or perhaps I should be either magnanimous or realistic and give Shakespeare all the credit. Whatever the case, we are all the "happy few" playing Harry.

"We Few, We Happy Few"

I learned from a middle-school English teacher that the speech did not die in fifth grade. One of my ex-students, whose attitude far exceeded her study skills, was in her class. When the class was asked what the meaning of the word "vile" was, they all sat there silently with that vapid look that we know so well. All but one. My little bad-attitude ex-student had her hand waving in the air. Having never seen this before, the teacher needed a moment before calling on her.

The eyes rolled, the head tilted, and the words "'Vile' means gross, disgusting, gag me with a spoon," came forth in a confident and rather annoyed voice. The teacher asked whether perhaps some cheating was involved, because how else would the girl know what that word meant? In this case, based on our experience of this student, it was a legitimate question. The answer was far from what the teacher expected. "*Henry V*, Saint Crispin Day speech. 'Be he ne'er so vile, this day shall gentle his condition.'"

The condition between her and the teacher gentled too, after that. There was an entirely new respect going both ways. I mean, the kid knew Shakespeare. Not only was she teachable, she was gentrified; that had to come with a bit of clout.

The teacher was kind enough to share that clout with me after the student told her she had learned *Henry V* in my class. Teachers love to share stories, and so I imparted to her how this very student had made me look like the village idiot and in the end I had to thank her for it.

The incident in question had been when my small group was being observed by a member of a school that focused on dropout prevention. We were one of their research schools. We were all seated, and the student, with her usual feisty mannerisms and rather colorful and occasionally painful way of expressing herself, raised her hand. I was almost afraid to call on her, but when the hand is being held two inches from your face, it is rather hard to ignore. I bit the bullet and called on her.

She informed me that Friday was October 25 and asked if we could have a party. My mind started to race as my face took on a blank stare. It wasn't Halloween… was it some new religious or ethnic holiday I wasn't up on yet? Okay, maybe she was just trying to play me. I tended to doubt that because what made her so lovable and forgivable was that she never lied and she never played those little games. So I just asked, "Why would we have a party on October 25?"

She gave me her best *God are you stupid or what!* look and threw in an eye roll for effect. "Friday, October 25, 1415. Henry beats the French at the Battle of Agincourt," she stated in a speaking-to-a-first-grader voice.

It took me a moment to wipe the egg off my face. I had to impress the woman observing me and made an attempt to look as smart as my student. "Okay," I said. "Well, it really isn't right to have a party for a battle." But, I explained, we had watched the battle scene from one movie and I had already explained how it was actually fought. So I said we could watch the battle scene from another movie and do a comparative study. As hard as it is to believe, the kids loved the idea. I was almost as floored as the woman observing.

She turned to me, leaned close, and asked "Is this the gifted program?"

I was beaming at each one of those kids as I said, "No, this is the dropout program." *We few, we happy few!*

A Little Touch of Shakespeare

Staying happy was difficult, as toward the end of my professional career Shakespeare got stuck to all that new red tape and couldn't be shaken loose. That is why, during a long-term special-ed inclusion subbing job, I took a shot and approached a very young, energetic, creative, and enthusiastic fifth-grade teacher. She was not a big fan of old Will, but she was a big fan of new ideas and of taking her class beyond what was printed in the classroom books.

The principal was just as excited about the program and she did everything she could to show her support. I wasn't just happy, I was in hog heaven. All of a teacher's hoped-for attributes either seeped into the students or they came that way, but they couldn't get enough. I went in during my free period, and what had been planned to be a few weeks turned into months. We watched *Henry V*, compared two versions of *Hamlet*, and we watched *Love's Labour's Lost.* Nothing was lost on them. Some went out on their own and bought DVDs of the movies. Others went as far as to buy DVDs and books of the plays, even ones we hadn't talked about.

I am a firm believer that you really can't get enough of a good thing. So I wrote a short script called *A Little Touch of Shakespeare.* The first setting is a classroom discussion about Shakespeare. It moves from that to scenes from the plays. My friend, that school's very talented music teacher, wrote the music for the three songs. I wrote the lyrics (thank goodness *he* was talented!). I resurrected the old costumes and got a local university to let us use their courtyard for one scene; the high school taped it, added background music, and edited. I was blessed with having a student who was actually a professional actor, and he read the lines like the pro he was. He became my assistant director. The parents were incredibly supportive and helpful.

A few of my happy few got to go to a board of education meeting, where they gave a brief live presentation and a preview of our DVD. One of my students was a bit nervous and asked me, "What if I forget some of the words to my speech?" He was doing the John of Gaunt death speech from *Richard II.* I told him to just keep going and that no one would know he had made a mistake, including me.

Love's Labor's Lost

I left at the end of the year and took Shakespeare with me. As far as I know, he still remains absent from the curriculum in all of the grammar schools. I want to apologize for being about as lengthy as one of Will's plays in writing about this. If "brevity is the soul of wit," then I am rendered witless. I only hope that some brave soul will pick up the pen *and* the sword—perhaps even a shovel—and do what it takes to resurrect Shakespeare once again. It's my dream, and unlike Mercutio in *Romeo & Juliet*, I hate to think that "dreams are the children of an idle brain." There is nothing idle or brainless about learning Shakespeare.

16

Native American Culture & the Environment

All my obsessions are not circumscribed by the history of across the pond. I do like to diversify occasionally. There is one such enthusiasm that I am not only completely devoted to and live my life around, but at times I have been known to find any excuse to force it on others. There is a part of me that is a die-hard environmentalist. I love, respect, and am in awe of nature, probably more than I am of most people. I have a sticker on the dashboard of my car that reads, "I'm a tree-hugging dirt worshipper." I also revere St. Francis and Buddha, who would both be pleased at how I pick up worms found dying on the sidewalk and move them to safety. Others just think I'm nuts, and I really don't care. After admitting this, I'm sure there will be those that wish I'd just stuck to England. If you really think about it, however, nature teaches us everything we need to know about living, even the qualities of being a good student.

It teaches us to look, observe, listen, and understand. It teaches us patience and the importance of sharing. It teaches us humility and caring. It teaches us the supreme lesson of cause and effect: consequences. One of our biggest problems with nature is that we just don't know how to connect to it, mostly because we don't bother to learn how to speak its language. So I try to teach how to form those connections.

The End of the Line for the Line

"We are line thinkers, but when it comes to our environment, we must learn to think in a circle. I will help to show you why and how." Though this may sound like an opening statement for one of those promotional books, it's how I begin to take my students on the road that leads back to them, which brings them back to nature. I use aspects of Native American Culture to do this. It has a great basis for connecting with nature. Why do the kids listen when I tell them to learn to think in a circle? Because I tell them how we eat our garbage. That bottle top, cigarette butt, napkin, bendy straw, and yes, even that dirty diaper sitting by the side of the road can come right back to us in what we eat. That is a real attention getter. They are then all ears to find out how to think in a circle.

The environment is, at best, a vague part of the curriculum in grammar school nor is it considered an important topic on testing. Native Americans are studied, but not with respect to their cultural relationship with Mother Earth. This type of life skill of relating to the planet is not included in the basic curriculum guide, so teachers allow me to sneak my program in while the kids are studying Native Americans.

"Circle thinking" is just another way of saying "cause and effect." A circle is easy to visualize, while "cause and effect" is an abstract concept, so the word "circle" works better. There are tons of concrete items to relate it with in our culture as well: the earth, the moon, and the seasons, to name a few. Don't forget, too, most living things are also round, including "us" (sometimes we're a bit rounder around the middle than we'd like to be).

As line thinkers, we sit in rows; our keyboards, digital clocks, streets, and even calendar are all in lines. After I point this out, the kids can "see" what is being said. When they see, they can relate. They can visualize our culture walking toward the end of the line and traveling on, never looking back at the effect of our actions, and then just dropping off when we get to the end. Remember when we used to think the world was flat? How archaic was that!

Our Outside Neighbors

They are now thinking and open to new ideas. I give them a question. I ask them why we call the animals that live outside "wild." After all, most animals kill or hurt for two reasons: food or fear. People, however, kill or hurt for food, fear, greed, power, jealousy, hate, and fun. "So, who sounds wilder to you?" Most get it and answer, "people." Now, they are a bit perplexed at how they have perceived things. Eyes are opening up to a new perspective on this thing we call nature.

Being passionate on the subject, I then talk quickly and constantly about how to relate to the environment through the ways of the Native Americans. I ask them questions like "Do you know what you can eat in your backyard?" and "Do you know what the healthiest plant is that you can eat, and unlike most plants, that you can eat every part of?" (It's the dandelion, by the way, just in case you didn't know—big surprise on that one.) I ask them to point south. Most point downward.

My ambassadors to the Native American totem animals are the ant and the skunk. The ant represents stamina and the skunk, respect and reputation. No way, Jose, you may say. Okay, well, just sit in one of those rows in the classroom for a moment and I'll give you the Readers Digest version: The ant can lift up to fifty times its weight. You can drop it from arm's height and it will walk away, which would be like us jumping off the roof of the school, or something even higher. And ants don't quit. The message: don't ever think you are too small to make a difference. Just keep trying, and like the ant, don't quit. (FYI, if you want to get rid of ants, forget all those harmful, expensive chemicals. Use baby powder. They hate it.)

What about that cute little waddling skunk? Point of reference: skunks have very poor eyesight and they are by nature nonaggressive. If you don't want to get sprayed, just stand still and don't make a sound. Nine out of ten times they will walk right by you.

Here's the example I give: A previous president of the United States stands in front of the class. Two Secret Service agents with guns are standing behind him. A tiger comes into the room. The Secret Service agents shoot him. A bear comes into the room. The Secret Service agents shoot him. A skunk comes into the room and everyone stands perfectly still, including the president. That's respect : when all you have to do is walk into a room and you have everyone's attention.

Ants and skunks are my favorite because I figure that if I can get kids to ease up on them, then all the rest are a shoo-in. For birds, try the crow or the pigeon. I'll let you look those up, but you'd be amazed what they can do. After giving students a brief "experience" with some neighborhood "wild" life, they get to close their eyes, pick a card with a picture of an animal, and look up its meaning.

Some Medicine Is Easy to Swallow

I give a general history of the totem bag and then the kids get to make their own. Taking a bit of creative license, I explain that "happy memory" items or the symbol of an animal totem that they feel close to go into the bag. It's not about expensive things. It's about personal things that are important only to them. Now they are connected in a kinesthetic way to the culture, to the environment, and to the circle that brings them back to themselves. One girl put this all together perfectly. She told of a day when her grandmother took just her to the beach. She smiled with her eyes as she recounted the day's details. At the end, her grandmother picked up a small shell and gave it to her because she felt that its beauty reflected the beauty of the child. It held the memory of the special day. Her grandmother had died a year later, she told us, but every time she looked at that shell she smiled and thought of that day. I tell that story to every group I speak to. You can hear a pin drop at the end.

My job is done if the students have learned about being closer to nature and caring for it. My job has a wonderful plus if I can get them to really think, to question, to see that there are many levels to things and watch the world get so much bigger in their eyes. I'm always surprised, too, by what I see. I get reports from kids about all the trash they picked up outside and how many birds, fish, and people they helped by doing that. Surprisingly, more often than not, it's the troublemakers in the class who really get into the message of the lessons. One class tormentor earned his way to becoming my helper in the other rooms by making totem bags. I guess everyone wants to connect to something, to believe that there's a personal message out there for them if only they look, and to feel special to something that is nonjudgmental. Nature doesn't follow our rules, and that could give them a new place to start. We just have to learn to "speak" the language of nature. It might be harder than Shakespeare's English, but it is the most excellent of languages and the most stunning way to communicate.

Maybe there is a little magic in making these bags. They were also known as medicine bags, and I guess they do carry a certain type of natural medicine in them. One natural item that was placed in the medicine bag was called a smudge stick. It was made up of dried sage and tied together with a string. It was lit and the smoke would be breathed in. It was said to help get rid of negative energy. Do I hear some snickering? Well, then, you probably never tried it. Fans of smudge never snicker, they just smile.

I don't smudge the kids at school, but we do it at Eco camp. Someone who was having a bad day would come to one of us and say he or she needed to be smudged. We would give some smudge and sympathy and the person left feeling better. Funny story: smudge when lit can unfortunately carry a similar aroma as another smoke that is connected with an illegal substance. This attracted the attention of the beach patrol officers who were stationed near our camp. We, of course, corrected the misunderstanding by showing them the "official" wrapper it came in (most health food stores sell smudge). We also offered them the opportunity to "be smudged." Some actually agreed, and a few came back when they were having bad days. Perhaps a medicine bag should be included on their list of equipment. They could use a bit of medicine and magic for what they have to deal with.

Magic or medicine (and probably far from authentic), it still amazes me what the program and the bags bring to the students and to me. If nothing else, it is a great model for explaining cause and effect and the impact of our actions, be it positive or negative.

It also teaches empowerment and control. What the students do or don't do can have an impact on themselves and their quality of life and on others. After all the years of doing the program, I've met students years later who make it a point to tell me they still have their totem bags. I've only had one student say that it would make a great case for his cell phone. Maybe he should have been smudged?

We really want to (and try to) make learning easy. I do it all the time. But what I noticed when I taught my obsessions with all my passion thrown in is that "easy" turned out not to be a factor. No one cared about easy. It wasn't even about fun, though it was *fun. Making the kids do hard work wasn't the point either, but they* were *working hard. There is a certain beauty and satisfaction that comes with working hard. It was about gaining knowledge for the sake of gaining knowledge. It had nothing to do with grades, scores, or rewards. There were no outside forces directing any of it. It was about learning a Shakespearean speech just to be able to recite it. It was about learning the history of English kings just because they lived. It was about learning how to think in a circle just to become part of the environment. Somewhere, someone once knocked on the door of inspiration for you and made you want to rush in and set up shop, too. It's wonderful to teach children what to learn, but it is so inspirational to share with children the love of learning.*

PART VII

It's all in the Presentation

*

Like a movie, it helps if what you're teaching has a good plotline.

17
Methods That Helped Me Teach

For the sake of brevity, time, and my self-esteem, I'm omitting the two-hundred-plus methods I tried that didn't work, or that I failed to use correctly, or that I just didn't like.

Please note: The following methods are also good for parents to use. It's okay to teach your children at home and have fun, and it's okay for them to feel like successes when slaving over homework. Just to prove that, I'll start with what I learned at home.

The Mother of Invention

My mother, like most women of her generation, was a housewife (or "domestic engineer," or whatever is correct now). She was also a great teacher, at least for me. She had an impeccable memory for "Well, when I was your age in school…" She would then call up some reminiscence of a class where she learned what I was learning. I don't know who her teachers were, but I thank them for their wisdoms. When I was given a spelling word list that consisted of the names of all our pertinent subjects, I was stuck on "geography" and "arithmetic." My mom came to the rescue with her "when I was your age..." teaching method. "Easy," she said, "just do what I learned to do—which is to take each letter and make a silly sentence with it." The silly sentence she learned for "geography" was "George Edward's old grandfather rode a pig home yesterday." For "arithmetic," it was "A rat in Tom's house may eat Tom's ice cream."

In high school, one of the vocabulary words I had to learn was "gamut." For some unknown reason, I got stuck trying to remember the simple definition that the teacher had given us. "Entire range" just wouldn't register into my memory bank until I decided to add a bit of music. My gamut mantra became "Home, home on the gamut, where the spelling and vocabulary plague." Obviously, these methods work—after all, I still remember them. By the way, does anyone have a sentence for "physical education?"

Acting

Teaching is very similar to acting. The major differences between successful teachers and successful actors is that successful teachers don't make tons of money and don't get to go on TV broadcast award shows. But they are required to do everything on one take and are responsible for all their own rewrites (and have to ad-lib when the script isn't working). The audiences are the toughest in the world, and a teacher rarely gets applause at the end of what might have been his or her greatest live performance. I've always wondered if actors can teach as well as teachers can act.

How many times will a child say something seriously, yet the entire class cracks up laughing? Teacher puts on the severest of expressions and preaches with the wrath of God, "Class, that was not funny!" knowing all the time it was downright hilarious. It was probably one of the funniest things she ever heard and behind that mask of rage she is side-splittingly, teary-eyed, belly laughing. But what isn't funny is hurting the child's feelings, which is what she was really saying.

Our best acting, though, actually comes when we're teaching the same old boring material. It can't help being boring by nature, because there's never anything too exciting about basic reading, writing, and math rules. Unfortunately, there isn't anything particularly memorable about these rules either, with the exception of the alphabet song.

When I was getting incredibly bored, never mind how the kids felt, I decided to think in a circle when teaching. I thought the students should be able to relate what they were learning to their "real" lives. So I decided to use all those tedious rules as my supporting cast. Kids relate to stories and emotions, not rules. So the rules took on personalities and feelings and the teacher was going to act them out. I decided to start my acting career with the syllable types. Some of the less-memorable rules are imbedded in the necessary evils, reading and spelling.

One of the other productions I created for reading lessons included a vowel cheer. There was also my personal favorite the story of Noah Webster which is great for all those exceptions in the world of reading rules. Now he becomes more than a dictionary author. He becomes our unsung hero. For writing lessons the lines on the paper become streets and the words become houses. Math problems become apartment houses, or even a trip to a middle school dance. There are so many stories hidden in those mundane rules.

Unfortunately, so many of the producers, directors, and financial backers of education have lost sight of the quality of the show and focus on the box-office take of how many kids will pass through the doors. They've even cut the running time of each production and are handing out preprinted scripts to all the cast of teachers. Gone is the independent production of academics. One show fits all, and there's not even time for a commercial break.

The impresarios have teachers and parents so busy looking at data and test scores that they forget that the best way to teach a child is to look at the *child*. You know...common sense. How does a child take in information? How does a child remember information? How does a child retrieve information? Why is the information important? Why should a child bother to learn it? How do we get rid of the fear factor? After all, learning and taking tests can get to be a real horror show at times.

18
Modalities

Know Your Audience

In the sixties, the popular greeting was "Peace, what's your sign?" Now the popular greeting is "Yo, whuz' up?" It would make life so much easier if a teacher could greet the class on the first day with "Good morning, what's your prime modality?" Of course, most children couldn't name it right off; most adults probably couldn't either, and let's face it, most people don't know what a modality is. Do you?

I never did, though like everyone else I use them all the time, for everything. You really can't do much without them. They are our prime modes, or ways, of learning. So where have they been hiding? Why don't we hear about them? They popped up a while back and were popular for a bit, but just like greetings, they went out of style and were lost on some dusty bottom shelf in the museum of the passé. I heard a rumor though that some systems may be dusting them off.

You might want to lend a hand to resurrect them, because they can help with teaching. What are they? The prime modalities of learning are seeing, hearing, and doing, otherwise known as visual, auditory, and kinesthetic modalities. See, wasn't that easy? We don't each use them equally, however. Some of us favor one (or even two of them) over the others. Lucky is the person born who is strong in all three.

Are you taking a little pause now to figure out what your strong modality is? Do you say about two seconds after meeting someone "I can't remember her name?" If you do, you can bet you're not auditory. Me? I can meet someone, leave the room, and hours later tell you what he was wearing, but not his name. Does that make me a clotheshorse snob? Not necessarily. (You'd know I'm not if you ever saw the way I dress…) It does mean I'm a visual learner who's the pits in auditory. You can talk me through four times how to use the computer and I just might get it. Let me do it as you're talking me through it though, and I'm a computer whiz (well, almost). So that means I'm also a kinesthetic learner. Take a moment and think about how you learn. Think about what you depend on to call up information.

Let me put it this way. If your friend is asking you for directions and is an auditory learner, give the names of all the streets to turn onto. If your friend is a visual learner, don't stop at just the names; describe the houses or buildings at the destination. If your friend is a kinesthetic learner, get into the passenger seat and give directions during the drive.

These methods can be translated to the classroom, as well. Say you are teaching a word to the class: reading it appeals to visual learners, saying it covers the auditory, and writing it is kinesthetic. Now, think about the students in your room and how they might learn. You can give them directions that will work for all of them. Most classroom teaching is presented in an auditory way. (By the end of the day, especially in the lower grades, we are so sick of hearing our own voices!) Visual is the next mode we use, and kinesthetic we use the least, especially as the grade gets higher.

If we teach to the modalities and give clues for each one, all students stand a chance of learning quicker and retaining more information. We also get to leave for the day without sounding so hoarse. It's not as complicated as it sounds or as time-consuming. Once you get in the swing of it, then it's like rote. Also, if you have students who are having difficulties, try to notice how they learn best, or just ask them.

Please keep in mind, too, those learning-disabled students. Just imagine what school is like every day when you learn best visually, yet your learning disability is in a visual area. It's a long, hard day. I always tell my new students, "The problem isn't that you can't learn. You can. The problem is that I have to find the way to teach you. It is my problem, not yours, but I need your help. You have to tell me what's working and what isn't and help me figure out the right way." They are usually so happy to hear that it isn't them, it's us, that they really try to help, because most kids really want to learn.

To connect with these three prime styles of learning, use the vast array of tools in your classroom creatively. Tape recorders (yes, some classrooms actually still have them) for the auditory, flash cards for the visual, math cubes for the kinesthetic. What about the computer? Computers can actually be good for all three and are exceptional for the visual and kinestic learner. What about games? Love them. What about framing academic rules with stories? This is definitely my favorite method. With a story, a child can mentally picture the clues and follow along with the plot. Sometimes we can manage to hit the visual, auditory, and kinesthetic in a single activity.

You can find more ideas on the Internet whenever you don't feel very creative. Try searching on "learning styles" or "modalities" for a start. Just remember: before we write a student off as a nonlearner or an apathetic learner, we must first accept some humility and say, "Maybe it's me." I'm a great teacher. I just have to find how to connect my greatness with how this student learns. Do I give him directions by street name, by describing the house on the corner, or do I sit next to him in the car and let him drive?

Happy trails, and peace.

19
Reading

. . . . .

Do We Ever Really Look at a Word?

Did you ever wonder where words come from? We say thousands of them over and over again every day of our lives. Some words are like old friends, cozy and familiar and we seek them out as much as possible, as with the word "Okay." Some people adore this word so much they use it as a verbal period at the end of a sentence. But does anyone ever stop and think where the word "okay" came from? Or for that matter, how we spell it. We have O.K. OK and Okay. Is it really acceptable or O.K., OK, Okay to have so many spellings of one word? I'm not here to answer that question, only to present it and make a point. The point is; where did the words that we read and spell come from and why do we constantly break all our rules for reading and spelling them?

The Mystery of the History of the English Language

William conquers England, and French and German get married.

Or

Why there are so many irregular words and exceptions to "the rules."

I usually start this part by instructing the class, "Raise your hand if English is your second language." A few reluctant hands go up. "Well," I continue, "you should be very proud of yourself, because English is the hardest language to learn." A big sigh of relief comes from not only the students who raised their hands, but also some students who have a hard time reading. This is a good time to state that teaching the history of the language and some of the other approaches to reading mentioned are actually helpful in teaching English as a second language.

Why?

Why is English the hardest language to learn? I explain that English doesn't really have a lot of rules, but it has tons and tons of exceptions to each and every one. It's enough to drive you crazy and make you want to cringe.

Why does English have so many exceptions to its rules? There's probably a multitude of reasons, but I like to stick to the basic two. The easiest explanation is that we don't say a lot of words the way we used to. Take the dreaded suffix "-tion." It used to be pronounced "ti-on." Over time, processed through various accents and whatever spirit moved them, people began to slur, drop syllables, and/or dabble in creative choices and changed pronunciations. Since a proper, official dictionary of English wasn't written until way after Shakespeare's time, spelling and pronunciation was up for grabs for a long time.

The most obvious example that can demonstrate to students how these changes take place is the "-ing" ending. Think about it. Even our presidents say "thinkin'," "talkin'," and "smokin' gun." One day, years from now, there will be a new rule—and it will be that we don't pronounce "the silent 'g'" at the end of "-ing" words. Just what we need…another rule.

The earliest explanation for the mystery in the history of the English language is from around a thousand years ago.

As the story goes

This is a very simplified version of the story. I mean very, very simplified. Linguistically, for example, there could be room for a bit of discussion over the function of multi consonants in a word. Historically all the Vikings and Romans, Edward the Confessor, bastard births, and Halley's Comet are left out for the sake of brevity (and censorship). All the specific rules and historical details can come later. Remember, this is not a college prep course. The point here is to get the students to really look at words. We are hoping to create an interest in understanding how words work, where they came from and let them breathe a sigh of relief that there is a method to the madness of reading and spelling.

Back in the year 1066, the country of England spoke a language that came from Northern Europe and the area around where Germany is today. This Germanic language loved consonants. The more consonants, they had the better the word. (You can show this by writing the word "right.")

Across the English Channel was a place called Normandy, which is part of France. Its people spoke an old version of French. The French love vowels. The more vowels, they had the better the word. (A lovely example to write for this is "beautiful.")

In Normandy lived a man named William the Conqueror. One rumor has it that he was a short, hairy, ugly guy (this description is always good for a "visual"), but he was a great and powerful ruler. William fell in love with a beautiful woman named Matilda. (This next part has nothing to do with English, but a lot to do with remembering about William and setting the scene for the lack of women's rights in eleventh-century Normandy).

William wanted to marry Matilda, but she kept putting him off because he was so short, hairy, and ugly (okay, that might be a stretch; I'm sure there was probably another good reason). One day he got so mad that as she was coming out of church, he pushed her down to the ground and insisted she marry him. Matilda said she would, but under one condition: he had to treat her with respect and as an equal. William must have really loved her, because he agreed, and he kept his word. When he went over to fight in England, he left her in charge of Normandy. Ruling Normandy was something that no woman had done before.

So, why did he go to fight in England?

William's relative, Harold, was king of England. But William decided that he should be king, so he got an army up, sailed across the English Channel, and started a fight at a place called Hastings. Harold got an arrow in the eye—ouch—and died. William became king.

Many of the Norman soldiers stayed and fell in love with and married the English women. When they got together, the German language that loves consonants and the French language that loves vowels also got married. That's how we got stuck with a language that is so hard to learn!

At the end, I tell the students that if English is their second language, they should pat themselves on the back for learning it. Half the class usually starts patting themselves on the back. They should, too. It's hard no matter who you are.

Your choice

If you are working with a group of students whose vague, vapid look persists as you tell this story with all your best acting ability, you might want to throw in the story of William's funeral. It could top any of Hollywood's horror movie endings.

William was extremely obese when he died. This wouldn't be a "huge" problem except for the fact that his body swelled up even more before getting him into his tomb. So, they pushed and they shoved him in and he burst! It's said that the only thing worse than the mess was the smell. Everyone made a quick exit from the funeral. You can pretty much guess that William the Conqueror will be remembered.

If you want to show some examples to get your students to look closely at words, you might bring up these examples:

from French	**from German**
see	right
tray	strength
bread	lamb
beautiful	knife
sneeze	high
believe	thought
been	knowledge
feathers	whistle
courageous	Wednesday
head	luck
language	would

I like to send the kids around the room, paper and pencil in hand, maybe in teams—to start searching for words for their own lists. They are on a mission. Maybe they're cheering for Harold, maybe William. Maybe all these words don't actually come from that particular story. It doesn't matter, at least not right now. What matters is that they are really looking at words. They are focusing on rules and what doesn't fit them. They are reading, and dare I say it, sounding out words!

Want them to run like the water through the room looking at words? Tell them the story of...

Noah Webster Spinning in His Grave
Learning irregular words and the exceptions to the rules

Strange as it may sound, sometimes seeing how a word doesn't fit a rule helps a student to learn the exception and reinforce the rule at the same time. Kind of like the two-bird-stone method.

A great, motivating story to get students to really look at words and see the challenge of the language is the story of our hero, Noah Webster. His portrait should be hung in every classroom. His name should be mentioned with praise and honor every day.

I'm not talking about the fact that he gave us our first American dictionary, or that he wrote one of first and most popular American spelling books (nicknamed the "Blue-Backed Speller"). This speller, by the way, is still in print today. He took on the insurmountable task of trying to get the powers that were to let us spell words the way they sound. Ben Franklin gave it a go once, but he wanted words spelled with all the odd letters and marks that symbolize sounds (the ones that come next to a word in its dictionary entry). Thank goodness that never happened. Noah wanted words spelled the way they sound, so, for example, "give" would be spelled "giv." All words would be phonically spelled, which would have brought an end to all irregular words. Just think what test scores would look like if they had let him have his way.

He did manage to get some changed. The British spelling of "colour" was changed to "color." The word "theatre" became "theater." His greatest quest was to get "-tion" spelled as "shun." That never happened, obviously.

Some background of the man is good to start with

1. He lived from 1758 to 1848 (though don't get bogged down with dates).
2. He was born in West Hartford, Connecticut. His family farmhouse is still there; tours are given. It's not far from the Mark Twain House and Harriet Beecher Stowe House.
3. He went to Yale.
4. He taught school.

One of the houses he lived in at New Haven, was on Water Street. It was the same house that Benedict Arnold had lived in. That house is now gone and so is the view of the water.

5. He used to grow peach trees in his backyard.
6. He is buried at Grove Street Cemetery in New Haven.

Starting the process

Show the students a picture of Noah's portrait. There are tons on the web. In the older classes, I include a photo of his tomb. Then write his name on the board. Under that, write it in syllables: "No-ah Web-ster." This makes it easier to say and remember.

Then send the kids on a quest to find all the words that make Noah spin in his grave. What words are these? Tell them that every time they find an irregular word or an exception to the rule, Noah gets so mad, he starts spinning in his grave. The more irregular the word, the more he spins. I usually have his portrait in my hand and start moving it around.

They will probably start by slightly turning their heads and searching with only a modicum of effort. Admit it; you might have a bit of difficulty spotting those words yourself. I did the first time

I went on the Noah journey. What words? Where? Well, they are all around you. They come at you every day and, like ghosts, we don't even notice. We are so conditioned to avoid real eye contact with them, they slip right by us like those speed limit signs on the highway.

So fasten your seat belts for an eye-opening spin.

Start with the number "one." Write it on the board (or if this is a personal journey, write it on a piece of paper).

What does the word say?

It says "one."

Wrong. It really doesn't say "one." We *know* it as "one." We *pronounce* it as "one," but if we are sticking to our rules, it says the sound that is in the word "bone."

If you want to really write it the way we pronounce it, you might spell it "wun."

Can you just see Noah (and maybe yourself) starting to spin?

Now, write the numbers "two," "four," and "eight" and see what they really say. How should they really be spelled? Ouch! Getting a headache yet? If not, I suggest try looking at the word "eye." That should do the trick and induce a need for aspirin.

Here are some examples you can use of how Noah, if he had succeeded, would have had us spelling some everyday words. Just think about how grades would go up and how much easier reading and spelling would be if they had just let us follow the rules! The current state of English is what happens when we borrow words from another time and country, but don't borrow the way they would say those words. I really hate when that happens.

Remember, don't be too hard on yourself or your students, and don't give up too easily. We are so conditioned to seeing words spelled and pronounced the wrong way that we think it's the right way.

If We Spelled It the Way We Pronounce It

(There could be more than one way to spell these)

the	(thuh)	they	(tha)	think	(theenk)
thing	(theeng)	do	(du)	laugh	(laf)
comb	(come)	come	(cum)	nation	(nashun)
earth	(erth)	neighbor	(naber)	find	(fiend)
minute	(minit)	could	(cood)	great	(grate)
right	(rite)	phone	(fone)	many	(meny)
have	(hav)	word	(werd)	bread	(bred)
school	(skool)	put	(poot)	what	(wut)

How about the word "have"? The "-ave" looks like it should make the sound like in the word "cave." In the words "think," "thing," and "find," the "in" looks like it should make the sound in the word "thin" and "fin" and "in." In the word "many," the "man" seems like it should really sound just like the word "man." Webster would say that part should be spelled "men," as in "more than one man." I guess you can say we've made a mistake and turned one man into *meny*.

As if this isn't bad enough, there are sounds that sometimes leave Noah smiling and other times spinning. They can change on a dime with no apparent rhyme (or is that "rime") or reason. I sometimes think of them as the moody rules. What they decide to say depends on their moods, like when you're looking over a menu and deciding if you're in the mood for pasta (posta) or pizza (peetzah).

Here's an example. Take the "ow" sound. "Ow" makes the same sound as "ou," which is the sound you make when someone pinches you. Ouch! Don't even ask why "ou" makes that sound; it's a whole other story. Unfortunately, sometimes "ow" makes the sound of a long *o*, as in "snow."

So, we have those nice, Noah's-smiling words.
Now how cow brow bow gown shower

Now, here's the mood swing and the spinning...
Snow tow crow blow bow grown show

Yes...did you notice "bow" and "bow"? Talk about moody! Reminds me of the words "wind" and "wind." Maybe they're not moody, but more like schizophrenic.

If Noah had had his way, we'd be spelling these the way they sound.

Sno to cro blo grone sho

(I *know*, you're looking at "to" and getting confused. We won't go there.)

What does all this bewildering spelling stuff accomplish? It gets students (and dare I say adults) to really look at words. It gets the students to set up a place in their heads where they can file all the words and the rules. It helps to really understand that, if you want to go by the rules, the English language is far from easy to learn. English is the king rule breaker of all the languages. So much for "long live the king."

We may feel we're going a bit over the top with all this, but kids love it. Send them on a mission to hunt down these words in the room, on a page, or on the computer screen, and they are good to go. Why? They get to do what every child (and some adults) loves to do most. They get to rat on every rule breaker they can find. They are the good guys on a quest for their hero, Noah Webster.

What this accomplishes for the teacher or parent is that they don't have to work at getting the kids to look at words. Students are sounding them out without being pushed. They want to learn the rules because they want to know who is breaking them. It also helps them to learn how to pronounce the rule-breaking words.

How to use "Noah Webster words" in reading, helping students to remember words and how to pronounce them

When the class is about to do a reading of a passage from any subject area, I pass out a paper with a portrait of Noah on the top (this is just for fun, but the portrait is not necessary to the lesson). What is necessary are the lines going across the paper. While the students read the passage they will write on their handout any word that they find important to the lesson, has some other noteworthy quality, one that they found difficult to read or just a good Noah Webster word. Once they finish reading, I ask for the words (I have a list prepared ahead of time in case they miss some) and I write each word on the board three ways:

1. The complete word
2. The word in syllables
3. The way the word sounds

Let's say the subject is social studies and we're doing a lesson on Ancient Egypt. The words on the board might look like this:

1.	pharaoh	phar-aoh	(fair-o)
2.	mummy	mum-my	(mum-me)
3.	pyramid	pyr-a-mid	(peer-uh-mid)
4.	regent	re-gent	(re-jint)
5.	dynasty	dy- nas-ty	(di-nas-te)
6.	research	re-search	(re-serch)
7.	machine	ma-chine	(muh-sheen)

Just a thought: you can combine this with the "mystery of the history of English" and point out Germanic- and French-based words. It all depends on what works for you and your class.

Here's the most important part for everyone to remember. Since English is the hardest language to learn, it only makes sense that it is the hardest to teach! So, to all you teachers, give yourself a pat on the back.

So What Are These Rules, Anyway?
And how come I didn't remember them?

If you stood outside any coffee shop and asked every mature adult who was about to walk in or out with an iPad or laptop or cell phone attached to their ear if they could name the six major syllable types or even what sound short *u* makes, I'll bet they couldn't tell you. I've tried it on professional adults, college students, even sixth graders—none of them had a clue. I didn't have a clue either until I learned it in some college course (or maybe it was even a workshop I went to). The point is, I knew I had learned the information once. We all have, but how come we can't remember it?

I thought about it. The only thing I could remember about the rules of pronunciation was about the double vowels: "the first one does the talking, the second one does the walking." That was it. So I decided that the syllable types needed a story for them to be memorable. They had to become human. They all had to learn to do some talking and walking. In other words, the syllable types needed to get a life. There had to be a plotline, heroes and villains, and somebody saving the day. And that's how the vowels became the heroes and the consonants became the villains.

Why?

Every word and/or syllable needs a vowel, but not every word and/or syllable needs a consonant. There are only five vowels. (Here's your first exception: The letters *y* and *w* are occasionally vowels, like in those moody "ow" words.) There are fewer vowels than consonants; they are the small but mighty. Plus, they can change their sounds, which is really hard for even just a few consonants to do. This makes them flexible, adaptable, and a bit magical and mysterious with perhabs a touch of alter egos, and secret idenities. It gives them the stuff that heroes are made of.

What are the six basic syllable types?

1. **VC** = vowel-consonant (short vowel sound) = at, it, up, pet, mop
2. **CVE** = consonant-vowel-*e* (first vowel has the long sound, second one is silent) = mate, bite, cute, mope, Pete
3. **VT** = vowel team (first vowel has the long sound, second one is silent) = aim, soap, meet, fuel, dial
4. **O** = open (a vowel at the end of a syllable that makes the long vowel sound) = be, no, ba-by, u-nit, I
5. **VR** = vowel-*r* (vowels take on new sounds before *r*) = far, fur, bird, her, for
6. **CLE** = consonant -*le* (the *le* has the "ull" sound) = circle, little, bubble, purple

- These are the basic syllable types and the sounds that vowels make. I'd start there. You can leave some things for later, like the gazillion-vowel combinations that are exceptions to these rules and the universal "schwa" sound (oy vey all those consonants! Talk about a Noah-Webster word).
- Just in case schwa does come up, because it's all over the place, you can call it "The Chorus." Schwa is the sound that every vowel can make. It's the "uh" that we know so well from the word "the" or "a." It's the sound all the vowels would make if they were in a chorus and had to sing the same note together. (I think *u* started it, so I would make him sing a little louder than the rest and on perfect pitch.)

The Lonely Life of a Short Vowel: The story of VC

Begin this lesson by writing the word "at" on the board. Then say: "It's a lonely life, being a short vowel. He has no vowel friends. The mean, jealous consonants block him in. Vowels, unlike people, can only move in one direction, left to right, so he can't escape. He can't move, he can't go out, he's so sad; he can't even say his own name." (This is a good time to look sad.) "Yes...it's a sad, lonely life being a short vowel."

Why are those consonants so mean?

At any time, you can explain why the consonants treat the vowels the way they do. If you don't explain it, there is a big chance that one of the students will ask you to. Give the reasons, explaining why the vowels are the heroes and so on, and tell the class that jealousy can make people and consonants pretty ugly.

Example:

cap,

up,

met,

mit,

top

Draw a sad face in or on the vowels

Ask the students why the vowels are sad (use your best sad voice). Have them repeat "Because he has no vowel friends." Now that they are completely depressed, add: "But wait!"

Secret Agent Silent E: The story of VCE

On the board, add an *e* to the end of the word "at" while saying: "Secret Agent Silent E sneaks in on the outside! He has to be quiet so the consonant doesn't see him, but the lonely vowel knows he's there and he's happy now. He has a friend. Even though they can't talk to each other, they look through the window and make faces at each other, text message, and smile. The vowel is no longer lonely. He's happy he has a friend, and he can say his own name now. He says 'ate.' Yippee!"

You can then add *e* to a few other words for practice and change the sad face of the short vowel to a happy face.

Example:

Cap (sad)	cape (happy)
Bit (sad)	bite (happy)
Mop (sad)	mope (happy)

Change the sad face on the first vowel and make it happy.

The Invisible Vowel: The story of VT

Write the word "team" on the board and say, "The invisible vowel is even more amazing. For some unknown reason, he is invisible to the consonants! He still has to be silent and not make even the smallest sound, but the vowel has a friend, up close and right by his side. He's so happy and he can say his name."

Make a smiley face on the letter *e* in team.

You can give another example by writing "ran." Then say, "Here's one of those lonely, sad, short vowels. Now, here comes the invisible "i."

Write in an *i*, turning "ran" into "rain." Happy days!

You can then do a few other words for practice

Example:

Man (sad)	main (happy)
Met (sad)	meat (happy)
Rod (sad)	road (happy)
Lid (sad)	lied (happy)
Full (sad)	fuel (happy)

Don't forget those little sad and happy faces on the vowels. They really go a long way to help kids remember.

- This could also be a good time to review that vowels, unlike people, can only move in one direction: left to right.

Life Is Good (or, Free to Be Me):
The story of O

Write the open-syllable word "me" on the board. Say, "This time the vowel is so lucky! There's no consonant to block her in. She can run like the water and go anywhere she wants, any time she wants. She's so happy she's just about shouting her name!"

You can then do a few other words for practice:

Example:

I	be
so	a

Make a smile face on the vowels, maybe one sitting on the top of "I."

The Consonants with a Heart: The story of VR

Write the vowel-*r* word "or" on the board. Say, "Some consonants can sometimes change their sounds when they get together, like *th, sh*, and *ch*. Some other consonants are pretty big hearted, understanding, and just don't hold a grudge. One of these consonants is *r*. When a vowel comes right before *r*, he just doesn't have it in him to be mean. The problem is, he just isn't a vowel, and as hard as he might try, he can only make the vowel a little bit happy. The vowel does appreciate his efforts and offer of kindness and is just happy enough to change her sound, but not enough to say her name."

You can then do a few other words for practice. (Don't forget the word "her" for starters.)

Example

for	sport
far	star
bird	third
turn	curb
her	germ

On the vowel r words I make a squiggly mark for the mouth instead of giving its face a smile..

The Mad E:
The story of CLE

Write the consonant-*le* word "little" on the board. Say, "The *e* should be open, but for some reason, the consonant and the *l* won't let that *e* run. The two of them together are very strong. They hold him back so he can just barely move! But the *e* doesn't get sad. Instead, it gets really, really mad! It gets so mad it won't say anything at all."

You can then do a few other words for practice.

Example

example	bundle
circle	sparkle
table	maple
boggle	little
middle	hassle

I put a straight line for the e's mouth.(Its lips are sealed.)

*Of course, always feel free to put as many words on the board as you want at the beginning and/or end of each lesson. It's also great to ask the students to give you a few. Sometimes they come up with some you would never even think of.

Remember, this is all made up. It's not a scripted lesson. You know the class and what works for it, so feel free to make up your own stories. I did.

Divide and Conquer

I should warn you. Dividing words into syllables can become a serious addiction. Okay, maybe it's closer to a mild obsession, if there is such a thing. Anyway, I do it all the time. When I have to learn someone's name, especially when I'm subbing or it's not a name I'm used to hearing, I start dividing it into syllables. If the name is really tough for me to remember, I divide it and spell it the way that would make Noah smile. When I have to address that person, I look in my head for those syllables and they seem to pop up quicker than the entire word. Who would have thought it?

Finding the little words in the words you divide is like one of those computer games you can't stop playing. You start looking everywhere for them: menus, street signs, junk mail. It becomes second nature, like covering your mouth when you sneeze or checking out your hair as you pass by a mirror. Well, there could be worse habits.

A few pointers and rule breakers to make syllables work for students.

1. You don't always have to start reading or spelling a word from the beginning of the word. Have students start with the part they know or recognize and then work the rest from there.
2. Every syllable has to have at least one vowel. If I write a multisyllabic word on the board, I sometimes underline the vowels so the students can get an idea of where those "little words in the word" might be or where to divide the word.
3. Just so you know, when you are dividing words by their internal sounds or looking for "little words," feel under no obligation to divide them the way the dictionary does. I don't.

Here are some of my favorites (I like to share). What I especially like about these is that you can start using them even in first or second grade (and go up from there).

independent in-de-pen-dent

It has three closed syllables, one open syllable, and four "little words": "in," "pen," "den," and "dent."

cooperate co-op-er-ate

There are four syllable types in this one. There's an open syllable, a closed syllable, a vowel-*r* syllable, and a silent *e* — not to mention the little word "ate."

attendance at-ten-dance

Here's a word used all through school at every grade. There are three closed syllables, a Noah Webster "ce," and three little words: "at," "ten," and "dance."

fantastic fan-tas-tic

This is what you say when everyone is getting the point. It has three closed syllables and three little words: "fan," "an," and "as." You can count "tic" as a word (as long as you add "tac" and "toe").

Here are some more you might like to use. There are lots of "little words" hidden in these. Have fun! (Clue: check out "elaborate.") I think this has some real potential as a word game.

Find the Hidden Words

teacher	subtraction	comprehension
electronic	understand	history
transportation	frustrate	devastate
elaborate	significance	carpenter

Vowel Cheer!

Since vowels are the key to turning letters into words, or make the world of reading and spelling turn on a dime (except when texting), they should be the focus of teaching letters. However, the alphabet song should not by any means be replaced. That has withstood the test of time (it seems even time is tested). Sing to your heart's content, and then when you're done singing, start cheering. There's nothing like a good cheer to get the blood flowing, the mind working, and the hands swinging.

The cheer is for the vowels. The teacher gets to be the head cheerleader (lucky you). Everyone stands in a line and the teacher faces the students. It has that "Simon Says" quality about it that makes it feel like a game.

Here's how the cheer goes:

Teacher: Give me an A!	(right hand on hip)
Students: A!	(hand on hip)
Teacher: Give me an E!	(left hand on hip)
Students: E!	(hand on hip)
Teacher: Give me an I!	(right arm held up bent at elbow)
Students: I!	(arm held up bent at elbow)
Teacher: Give me an O!	(left arm held up bent at elbow)
Students: O!	(arm held up bent at elbow)
Teacher: Give me a U!	(both hands on shoulders)
Students: U!	(both hands on shoulders)
Teacher: Whaddayah got?	(both arms held high)
Students: Vowels!	(both arms held high)

(Repeat last two lines.)

A few small comments:

The students will probably lift their opposite hand and/or arm, since they are facing you. This need not be an issue unless you want it to be. Also, notice the rather slang ending phrase "Whaddayah got?" which is very grammatically incorrect, but this is poetic license. It just sounds more like a cheer. Please, by all means, if you find this offensive make the correction. You are also entitled to change any hand and arm positions, or throw in some dance steps, pom-poms, acrobatic maneuvers—whatever floats your boat and the class's. Remember, this is your show, so go for it!

The really fun part comes right after they learn the cheer. Now you can really make a game out of it: move your arm to any letter's position and they have to call it out. A student taught me this… though not on purpose.

I was working with a small group of students who needed vowel reinforcement prior to some major testing. I did the cheer. They liked it. They got to stand, move their arms around, and yell sounds. What's not to like? One student was so excited that she finally knew her vowels. She asked if I would go back to her room with her so she could say them to her teacher. Why not? I love being the bearer of good news.

The problem was, by the time we got back to the room, the fear factor had escorted her to the door and she went blank. I stood behind the teacher, facing the girl with a big smile on my face and my right arm high in the air. She returned the smile and said the letter *A*. I went through the motions as she named each vowel. A good time was had by all, except the Fear Factor. He went to time-out.

If the group is really into it, you might want to experiment with substituting the vowel's name with its short vowel sound. Just might be worth a try.

Finger Spelling
A picture may be worth a thousand words, but sometimes the best way to read it is with the language of the hands.

Many years ago, I noticed that Yale University was offering a free, unaccredited course in American Sign Language. Two things appealed to me right off: it was free, and unaccredited. If I didn't like it, I could just walk away, no harm done. As it turned out, I really enjoyed the course. I took my book home and studied. I didn't know any deaf people to try out my new form of language with, so I decided to show off with my students at school. I would sign "very good" when they got something right, "yes," "no," "good morning," and such things through the course of each group. They thought it was fun and learned to sign back.

I got very creative with my new skill when the music teacher, who was legally deaf and had hearing aids, was doing the Christmas concert. I convinced her that when her group of students sang "Silent Night," I would have a group of students signing the song. I didn't choose that song because of its religious connotations; I just thought the title was a good tie-in for the signing event. She loved the idea. So, with her conducting the *singers* and me conducting the *signers*, we put on our performance for the school. We got rave reviews from staff and students, which went directly to my head and left me yearning for signing situations.

As luck would have it, the next year I had a small group of students who were bombing in reading. They had had it. They knew they were flunking reading and had given up on even trying. As far as they were concerned, phonics was some foreign, bitter raw vegetable that they wanted no part of. They moaned. They groaned.

They talked in class. They almost ignored me completely. So one day, at wits' end, I told them that we were going to forget about reading and phonics and spelling. We were going to learn to talk to the deaf. We were going to learn how to finger spell. We were going to learn something that nobody else in the school knew how to do, like a secret code language.

They loved the idea, especially since I had told them we weren't going to be doing reading or spelling. I loved the idea too, because I could use at least part of my sign language skills. When they looked down at the words on a sheet of paper or a page, all the letters looked the same to them, the sounds were the same, and so were all those tedious rules, but the hands… the hands flew and curved and bowed in fluid contortions through the air, teaching them the basic skills. It was, for me, the perfect and universal way to teach. It covered the visual, the auditory, and that ever-neglected modality, the kinesthetic. With the kinesthetic, the students' hands became a personalized computer memory chip. If they forgot a sound of a letter, I would tell them to finger spell it. When they did, the sound came back to most of them, popping into their heads and right out of their mouths. I was just as amazed as they were at how well that worked and had no real explanation for it. Sometimes, I think, it's best to leave a good mystery just that: a good mystery.

Who would have thought that the one course that was the biggest help in teaching kids reading and spelling I didn't have to pay for and didn't get any credit for? I didn't even have to take a test for it. When you think about it, my students when learning reading and spelling were also free, perhaps not just of payment, but of judgment. They didn't get credit on their transcripts for the language of the hands, nor were they ever tested on it. I guess what comes around, goes around. (I know it's really "what goes around, comes around," but sometimes it's fun to change things around… and around and around.)

By the way, did you notice that "singing" and "signing" have the exact same letters and that they are both Noah Webster words?

Remember, we're not kids anymore. Sometimes we find learning something unorthodox like finger spelling a bit tedious or even scary. If you want to escape the monotonous and face your fears, give it a try. When you use it with your students, just spice it up and make some modifications for memory skills. I deviated a bit from the authentic method. Please make note of this, because finger spelling professionals might give you an odd look as your hands dip, swing, and shoot forward at some pretty strange (but not obscene) angles.

Learn the finger positions one step at a time

The first thing you are going to need is a finger spelling chart. You can get them from books and there are tons on the Internet.

Finger spelling is not only good for teaching sound-symbol association but also letter sequencing, kinesthetic learning, focusing, memorizing sounds, and fun. It's also good for higher-grade students. It's hard to get older students to learn skills that you and they know they should have learned years ago. Some of them never caught on. Some of them learned a thing once, but then it went the way of the dodo. Some of them just need a bit of review. Finger spelling is like sidestepping the obvious. They can avoid the notion that they didn't learn a skill and focus on learning a new way of communicating.

The method is easy enough to modify to use for teaching reading and spelling rules. One actually reinforces the other. You can tell the students that they are learning how to talk to the deaf. You're not lying; you're just omitting the fact that it's helping them learn their own lessons. The point is, they aren't stepping backwards but moving forward. It's a good place to move to.

Making the letters

Hand placement:

Place your hand by the side of your face and have students do the same. This position is used when speaking to the deaf so that they can also read lips. It works well for any student because the focus stays on the face of the person who is finger spelling.

Teaching the Letter Sounds

- When teaching the finger positions, always use the sound that letter makes and not the name of the letter.
- Always teach the sounds using word families,(such as at, un, eat, ink, ock,) not by going through the alphabet.
- You do not have to teach all the letters at once. Usually it is best to use word families that have the most common letters. You can introduce letters as the need arises (like when you come across words with *qu*, *z*, or *x*.
- Remember, Rome was not built in a day, and neither is learning to finger spell. Do lots of review and don't rush to introduce too many new letters at once.

Example:

Make the hand position. Tell students the name of the letter and then the sound of the letter (from then on, when finger spelling words, just use the sounds).

I start with the short vowel sound of the letter *a*. (You can also write it on the board.)

4. Place hand near face and make the *a*.
5. Say, "This is the letter *a*."
6. Have students make the letter.
7. Then say the short vowel sound and have them repeat it.
8. Do this a few times for reinforcement.

Next, show them the letter *t* and repeat the steps. Once they have practiced, show them how to finger spell the word "at."

After some practice, show them the letter *b*. Say, "This is the letter *b*. You know how to finger spell 'at.' Can you make the word 'bat'?"

After some practice, show them how to finger spell *c*. Say, "This letter is *c*. Can you finger spell the word 'cat'?"

Continue by just changing initial consonant sounds: try *f*, *h*, *m*, *p*, and *s*.

You can then choose to change the vowel sound, the final consonant sound, or both initial and final consonant. Choose according to how you like to teach, the skills you're working on, and/or according to the class. You can always introduce a new letter and show the students how to make it: "You know how to finger spell 'mat' and 'pat.' Can you finger spell 'map'?" Or, "This letter is an *n*. Can you finger spell the word 'nap'?" Don't forget the vowels:

"This letter is an *i*. You know how to finger spell 'bat.' Can you finger spell the word 'bit'?"

.....

Note: the below methods deviate from finger spelling rules. I made them up, so they are not official. You can change any of them and make up your own. The most important thing is to be consistent and have the students practice.

Long vowel sounds:

These can be introduced while teaching the short vowels or after; it's your choice. Just make sure the students are comfortable finger spelling three-letter words.

When finger spelling words that contain silent *e* or vowel teams, place the index finger of your other hand to your lips (like a "shhh" gesture) when you come to the letter that is silent. When you do this, the students should make the silent letter with their other hands but not say its sound.

For example, make a short-vowel word, such as "bit," then the long-vowel word, "bite." Others are:
cap/cape
mat/mate
mop/mope
hop/hope
cut/cute

Follow the same procedure with vowel teams within words. Make a short-vowel word such as "got," then the long-vowel word "goat." And so on. Others are:

red/read
bat/bait
plan/plain
men/mean
rod/road

If there is a vowel team with two of the same vowels, such as in the word "feed," or a double consonant as in the word "fill" you can nod your signing hand up and down while you're saying the sound.

Open syllables

In an open syllable, the vowel is long. To show this, I do what I call a "slide." Make the vowel, sliding your hand off to the side as if it is running away. I do this to show that there is no consonant blocking the vowel, so it can make the long sound.

Vowel*-R *sounds

When a vowel is followed by an *r*, the sound of the vowel changes. To show this, I do what I call "pushing forward." Make the vowel, and then as you make the *r*, move your hand forward.

Blends & consonant*-le *sounds:

Two consonants coming together to make a blend change their sounds a bit. To show this, I do what I call "dip and rise"—dipping the hand for the first letter and raising it back up for the second letter in the blend. You can also use this for *qu*.

Digraphs

In digraphs such as, *ch, sh, th, wh*, and *ph*, the consonant sounds change. To show this, I do what I call "shooting dice." For the first letter, move the hand upward, then as you quickly shoot your arm downward (as if shooting dice), change to the second letter.

There are ways you can reinforce the skill of finger spelling:

1. Finger spell a word without saying its sounds and have students figure out what it is.
2. A student can do the same as above for other students to answer.
3. Write some words on the board and see who can finger spell them.
4. Finger spell a blend, digraph, or silent *e* and see how many words they can come up with that uses it. Have the student who comes up with a word finger spell it to the class.
5. I'll bet you can come up with even more ideas!

Let's face it, when did you ever think that hand gestures would be something you would use for teaching?

20
Streets & Houses

Streets and houses (not to be confused with Chutes and Ladders) can be used as an easy tool for teaching a variety of subjects. My favorite locations on the academic road map of skills are writing and math. I had to become relatively desperate to teach a subject to come up with the idea. It is, however, something that all kids can relate to. They all know what a street is and what a house is, for be it ever so humble (or messy), there's no place like home.

On the road again...

Writing

Nearly every grammar school teacher (and a few from the upper grades) has had students who just don't get the special relationships between the different symbols we use in writing. If only the paper-and-pencil routine came with that wonderful, long and mighty space bar, like a keyboard. But it doesn't. So when we told the students that there's a space between two words, the word 'space' seemed to be out there, somewhere far, far away...like outer space.

Consequently, "I like to play ball after school." ends up looking like "Iliketoplayballafterschool."

Have you ever noticed how teachers are the best at those e-mail quizzes, word searches, and even my forte, Boggle? Well, this is why. They have spent years searching for words on students' papers.

The clue is to get rid of the word "space" in the directions. Leave that to the computer and the planets. Instead, the lines on the paper become "streets." They are all one-way streets that go from left to right (a little one-way sign with an arrow at the top of the paper can help). On the streets are houses.

On the board, write the word "I" and tell the kids that in the first house lives the "I" family. There is only one person in this family (and he must be pretty lonely sometimes), but it's a small house and looks cozy. Then draw a roof over the word "I." You can add a chimney and some smoke for a little effect to help the visual learners and just to add humor for those who enjoy a laugh as they learn.

The "like" family lives in the next house. There are four people in this house. Write the word on the board and give it a roof. I generally write the number of letters in the word over the roof. Leave a "space" between the houses, of course, but don't name it. Once the house is in place, announce that you had to leave a yard or driveway between the two houses. That way, the people in the house can fit a car there and they can look out a window and have a bit of a view. The best way to have enough room for the car is to use one finger between the two words. If you want to extend the example, write the two words without the space first and say what an awful problem that is, because some people are in someone else's house instead of their own. (If you're in the mood for drama, you can make up a story of how the "like" family doesn't really get along with "I" because he's always complaining that they are too noisy and "I" is the last person they want in their house.)

You can follow that story line to build the rest of your sentence ("I like [...]) until you get to the period, which we call the "stop sign." Explain how there is a stop sign between two crossing streets. You stop because you don't want to get hit by another car. If you still follow the old method of two finger spaces after a period, question mark or explanation point, you can say that it is a two way street and two fingers spaces instead of one is needed for two cars to fit.

Cars are the size of fingers. Letters live together as families on streets made of lines. Sure, in the beginning, you will get back papers with roofs on the words, chimneys, and perhaps little drawings of trees, dogs, and flowers in some of the spaces, but eventually they dwindle away and the space remains intact. And we will all make fewer trips to the eye doctor in need of stronger glasses.

I do suggest that you not use this method if you are being observed, especially if the observer has no idea what the process is. It can be cause for some concern if the supervisor sees you walking around the room pointing to papers and asking your students "Are you sure there's enough room after that stop sign?" or hears you say "The 'play' and 'baseball' houses have a pretty small driveway. They could never fit a car in there." The supervisor may think you are teaching a civil engineering course to your second graders, that you are filled with delusions of grandeur, and not only that, but she is pretty sure civil engineering isn't on the mastery test. Not good for evaluation reports. Just a thought.

Math

Sometimes the processes of carrying and borrowing become confusing for certain students. It could very likely have to do with conceptualizing the process or simply figuring out how to remember them. These kids need a story. You don't have to start with a "Once upon a time," but if you want to teach place values, then give the numbers a place to dwell. For carrying in addition, the dwellings are one-family houses. For borrowing in subtraction, the dwellings are apartment houses.

Addition

In addition, carrying is the big rule of the neighborhood, and the other rule is that there can be one- or two-family houses on the left side of the street but only one-family houses on the right side.

For example, the sum written "68 + 48" lengthwise looks like this on the "street map":

$$\begin{array}{r} 68 \\ \underline{+\ 48} \end{array}$$

Tell the students to think of this arrangement as a street. You can draw a "center line" (vertically, just to the left of the digits on the "right side of the street") that extends down through the horizontal line between the two rows that extend down past the bottom line, if that helps as a visual aid. Then tell them the other big neighborhood rule: students have to add up the number of houses on the right first and see if any have to go across the street.

They add the 8 + 8, which equals 16. Place the numbers under the bottom line. Oh, no! There's an extra number: the 1. The 1 has just broken the zoning regulation for the neighborhood. Oh well...that 1 has to move across the street. The 1 builds a house above the 6. There's a big send-off party on the right side and a huge, welcome-to-the-new-neighbor potluck dinner on the left side.

Now the street looks like this:

$$\begin{array}{r} 1 \\ 6\,8 \\ \underline{+\,4\,8} \\ 6 \end{array}$$

Even though it doesn't matter to the zoning committee if there are more-than-two-family houses on the left, you may think you don't have to add up the left side. Not so! The census taker is coming around and all the houses have to be counted. So the left side needs to be added up, too. 1 + 6 + 4 = 11. Which leaves the answer:

$$\begin{array}{r} 1 \\ 6\,8 \\ \underline{+\,4\,8} \\ 1\,1\,6 \end{array} \qquad \text{Voilà!}$$

Subtraction

For borrowing, the street is gone and so are those little one- and two-family houses. This is a more urban setting. Now, we're talking about apartment houses.

For example, the difference written lengthwise as "45 – 28" would look like this on the street:

$$\begin{array}{r} 4\,5 \\ \underline{-2\,8} \end{array}$$

Tell the students to think of this arrangement as an apartment house. There are two floors and four apartments. You can draw a line down the middle to show the hallway between the two sets of apartments. On the right side of the hallway live the "1" families. On the left of the hallway live the "10" families. Lots more people are crammed into the left side than the right.

There is only one big rule for living in this apartment house: "There must be more people living on the top floors than on the bottom floor." If you have fewer people in your top-floor apartment, you're kicked out, evicted, homeless...out on the street with no TV, computer, bed, cell phone—and worst of all, no bathroom. (Well, you get the idea.)

So, let's look at the "1" families. Oh no, bummer! It looks like if the 5s don't do something quickly, they are out on the street. They run across the hall to where the "10" families live, and luckily they get along pretty well. They explain the situation and ask one of the "10" families to join them across the hall and they are really open to the idea. After all, they have four families of ten people living in their apartment and it is pretty crowded. So it's a win-win.

So, a family of 10 packs up and moves across the hall. This is when the 1 is written in front of the 5 and the students are told, "Okay, there's a new family of 10 in here, plus the 5, so there are 15 people living there now. Across the hall, everyone is happy too because there's one less family living there. So now they're down to 3 families." This is when you cross out the 4 and write the number 3 above it.

Now, to make sure everything is on the up and up, the landlord comes over to check exactly how many more are living on the second floor than the first. This landlord is really tough, and you don't want to mess with him when he gets like this. Okay, so 15 – 8 = 7. The

"1" side of the apartment house is safe! On the "10" side there are 3 families – 2 families = 1 family. They are safe too! Whew.

$$
\begin{array}{r}
45 \\
-\ 28 \\
\hline
17
\end{array}
$$

The answer for the landlord is that there is a total of 17 more families on the second floor, so nobody gets the boot.

This may all sound completely ridiculous to you. If you have a better idea, go for it. But to my surprise, I found this method really worked when reviewing arithmetic with middle school students. I think it helped pull up and reinforce what was tucked somewhere in the backs of their minds. It was silly, so it wasn't completely boring. The point is, not all children learn the same way, and we should give them options on the road to knowledge. The more a lesson relates to them and their lives, the easier it is for them to remember.

Perhaps you have a valid argument that this really isn't teaching place value, and you are probably correct. I say that for some children, it is so much more important, first and foremost, that they *know they can learn*. Once the confidence is there, then the mind is open to take in "The Secret Legend of Place Value" and "The Lost Treasure of Number Concepts." I'll let you make up those two on your own.

21
More Math

Nine, the Math Motivator

"The whole nine yards," "dressed to the nines." "a stich in time saves nine." Who knows where these expressions came from or what they really mean? One thing about "nine" is that it is the best number to teach any child who is afraid of math. I love nine. It's the magic number of math. It is every simple man's "pi" filled with amazement and wonder.

Nine in multiplication and division

I didn't realize this until I started teaching and some very thoughtful comrades were kind enough to show me the "nines table" tricks. I was in awe and loved to see the awe on the kids' faces when they learned it. So, if any of you were never privy to the secrets of the nines table, here it is.

Place your hands, palms down, on a flat surface (or in the air, or on your knees, wherever). First, let's take "9 x 2." Start counting with the little finger of your left hand. When you get to the next finger (the "second" finger, because we're doing nine times *two*), bend it at the knuckle. Now, count all the fingers on the left side of the bent finger: 1. Now, count all the fingers on the right side of the bent finger: 8. Your answer is 18.

Want to try it again? Let's do 9 x 8. Start counting with the little finger of your left hand, going to the right until you get to "8." Bend that finger. Now, count all the fingers to the left of the bent finger (7) and all the fingers to the right (2). Your answer is 72. Who needs a calculator?

It doesn't stop there. When I teach the nines table, I tell the students I can show them a way to learn it in two minutes. "Yeah, right, lady," is the look I get most often. I then smile and begin my story: "Billy's teacher spent an entire week teaching her class the nines table. Unfortunately for Billy, he never bothered to pay attention. The day of the test came. The teacher told the students to write the equations and the answers for '9 x 2' through to '9 x 9' along the side of their papers." This is when I write these equations on the board. "She then told them to count the ones they think they got right and put that number on the top of their papers. Billy wrote the examples down and said to himself, 'I don't know any of these. I'm better off just counting the ones I got wrong.' And so Billy started to count them up."

Here's where I pretend to be Billy and start writing on the board:

9 x 2 = 1	"There's one I got wrong."
9 x 3 = 2	"There's two I got wrong."
9 x 4 = 3	"There's three I got wrong."
9 x 5 = 4	"There's four I got wrong."
9 x 6 = 5	"There's five I got wrong."
9 x 7 = 6	"There's six I got wrong."
9 x 8 = 7	"There's seven I got wrong."
9 x 9 = 8	"There's eight I got wrong."

"But," Billy goes on to say, "I'd just better make sure and count them again. I'll start at the bottom and count up so I don't make a mistake." I start with the 9 x 9 = 8 and place a 1 next to the 8 and say "There's one 1 got wrong." I continue counting and saying how many were wrong, and by the time I get to the top, it looks like this:

9 x 2 = 18
9 x 3 = 27
9 x 4 = 36
9 x 5 = 45
9 x 6 = 54
9 x 7 = 63
9 x 8 = 72
9 x 9 = 81

And Billy says "I guess I got them all wrong, so I'll put a big zero at the top of my paper." By now, most of the kids recognize some of the examples and realize he actually "got" them all right. I call out to the class, "Did he get them all wrong?"

And they call out, "No! He got them all right!"

You don't have to stop there. The magic of nine has just begun. I tell them (always tapping the chalk on the board—or the marker, if it's a whiteboard), that the answers to these equations with nines always add up to nine: 1 + 8 = 9, 2 + 7 = 9, and so on. So, if the answer doesn't add up to nine, you know it's wrong.

I then tell them that 18 is written as the "opposite" of 81, 27 the opposite of 72, and so on. Not only that, but to find an answer from the nines table if you don't have them all in front of you is also very easy. Just subtract 1 from the second number and subtract that answer from 9:

9 X 2 =	take 1 away from the 2 and you have 1	9 X 2 = 1
9 X 2 = 1	take that 1 away from 9 and you have 8	9 X 2 = 18
9 X 3 =	take 1 away from the 3 and you have 2	9 X 3 = 2
9 X 3 = 2	take that 2 away from 9 and you have7	9 X 3 = 27
9 X 4 =	take 1 away from the 4 and you have 3	9 X 4 = 3
9 X 4 = 3	take 3 away from the 9 and you have 6	9 X 4 = 36

And so on.

There are so many ways that the nines let you teach with such ease. It's almost heartbreaking when the students realize all the other numbers aren't as agreeable as the nines. The nines please, they comfort, they place smiles on future (and even not-so-future) mathematicians. It's the number that just doesn't stop giving. Even in division, the nines climb to the highest power of ease. Division is even easier than multiplication. Watch this:

18 divided by 9 (just add a 1 to the first number) = 2
27 divided by 9 (just add a 1 to the first number) = 3
36 divided by 9 (just add a 1 to the first number) = 4

I could go on for hours, but you get the picture. Oh, if just everything in life could be this easy. What I really like is when students start looking for patterns or clues for working with other numbers. They may not come up with any, but they start thinking about math, how it works, how numbers interact with each other. They see relationships and configurations. Some come to realize that everything is really working off of 10. If they don't see it, if you give them some clues they are more interested in hearing about it. They want to learn; they just want it to be easy. In their quest to find what is easy, they end up grasping the concepts of math. Above all, nine is the math motivator and the terminator of the fear factor.

Adding and Subtracting with the Nines

I was never taught an easy way for adding and subtracting with the nines. Years ago, I had a student who was incredibly smart and just as incredibly learning disabled when it came to math. By fourth grade, he still did not have the slightest idea how to add or subtract past the number 10. For him, number processing might as well have been translating the Mayan calendar. I had "15 – 9 = " written on the board. We both stared at it. He was feeling very stupid because the answer was nowhere in his memory bank. I was feeling very stupid because I couldn't find a way to teach him.

I took what I knew. He was smart. I needed a process, a method—no matter how off-the-wall—that he could follow. From my work with the nines in multiplication and division, I was secure in the fact that nine was magic, so I did what I tell students to do. I stared at the example and looked for some type of pattern. It came to me. It had been staring at me the entire time. I didn't know why I didn't think of it before (like thirty years ago, when I could have really used it).

I went up to the board and told my student to add the 1 + 5 in the number 15. He said "6."

I said, "That's your answer." I don't know who was more thrilled, him or me. It was a real toss-up on that one. "Yes," I stated, "all you have to do is add the two top numbers together to get your answer. Well, at least it was true for numbers between 10 and 19, but that's where we started. He enthusiastically wrote every one of them up on the board and whipped through answering every one of them with great speed and confidence.

I knew we were on a roll, and together we came up with subtracting 9 from numbers greater than 19. So, "24 – 9 = " was put on the board. We studied it with dignified contemplation and found the way. Take the 1 from the 2 in 24 and put it on the bottom line, then add that 1 to the 4 and you get 15.

For addition we did just the opposite. We wrote "3 + 9 = " on the board. So, add a 1 to the bottom under the line and then take that 1 away from 3, which gives you 2. From that you get an answer of 12. If one of the addends is a double-digit number, as in "13 + 9 = ," then add a 1 to the 1 in 13, which is 2, and then subtract 1 from the 3, which is also 2: your answer is 22.

Sound complicated? It is until you start doing it. Remember, this boy was smart, but due to a learning disability he could not approach math the way it was usually taught. He was so smart and became so confident that he came in one day and told me he had figured out how to do a pattern with the 8's and so on down. It was all based on the number 10. (I was really impressed and had him explain it to me a few times so I would get it…) In all fairness, all this is easier to explain with a student at the board than it is to write it down like this in a book. It just comes across better verbally, with visual aids and kinesthetic hand movements going across the board.

Still, I am telling you, it just might work with certain students. It worked with this one. He was smiling. He could do math. He couldn't wait to come in for math. He loved math and he was passing it. The block was gone, the fear factor relocated, and he was zipping down the road of numbers. So I won't make any apologies. Sorry, about that but I won't.

War Games

Nowadays when kids want to carry around their games, they bring some small, computerized mechanism. My friends and I used to carry around decks of cards. If you do find a deck tucked away in the back of some drawer, it might be time to pull it out again, dust it off, and start playing "math war."

I wasn't going to include this in the book at first, because it can be difficult to use with an entire class, but it can work if played in teams, with lots of enthusiasm and various certain modifications. It does work really well with small groups—and best as a game parents can use at home in lieu of flash cards. I know this because, along with playing it at school, I started playing it with my five-year-old nephew. He loved it, and he's learning math at five! Who would have thought?

Addition

Card values

Each pip card has its corresponding number value. You can assign aces, kings, queens, and jacks any number value you want according to the students' grade level. For example, if you are doing addition with numbers only through the 30s, then use the kings, queens, and jacks for those numbers. For lower grades, I have aces be ones or elevens, and the face cards are just more tens.

How to play

Place one card in the center. This is the addend card for everyone. If you are working on an addend of, say, four, then place a 4 card in the center.

Pass the rest of the cards out to the students.

Each student turns over a card and adds its value to the center card's value.

The one whose sum is the highest wins the pile.

If two or more students turn over same-value cards, they call out "war" and each turn over one more card to see who gets the higher one and wins.

When all cards have been used, the students count their cards. The one with the most cards wins.

If you want to do a general review of addition, do a version where you don't place a card in the center but instead have each student draw two cards, add them together, and see whose sum is the highest.

Adding with more than two numbers

You can even extend the game to adding three or four numbers together. For a classroom setting, have two teams. One student from each team stands at the board. Another from each team stands at the front of the room with a deck of cards and they turn over two cards each. The students at the board write down their team's numbers (or the whole class can write them down on paper) and add them. You comment on who is winning so far and how many more points one team has than the other—however far you want to stretch it. The third card is then turned, which determines who the final winner is. You can rotate students from each team to come up to the board and to turn the cards.

War pointers

Why "math war" is better than flash cards:

1. It's fun.
2. There are as many clubs, hearts, diamonds or spades illustrated as the number on the card. If the child doesn't know the answer have them say the highest number out loud and then continue counting while touching each club, heart, diamond or spade on the other
3. Adding with 10s is the easiest. If the player doesn't know the answer, just cover the zero of the 10 card with the number on the other card and show it to him or her.

Multiplication

This is basically the same as the addition version, but instead, you multiply.

There, wasn't that easy?

What's Your Angle?

I was subbing in a fourth grade. The kids were great, if you overlooked the fact that sitting still and more than a five-minute attention span were nonexistent. But they weren't malicious. They were fun loving, showed signs of really wanting to learn, and had a great sense of humor. It was right after lunch (bad time of day) and we were to begin math. I checked over the required scripted lesson. It was on acute, right, and obtuse angles. The lesson looked pretty obtuse to me, and I knew teaching this for forty-five minutes was going to be an exercise in futility. I really hate those exercises. They can be very painful.

I gave it some deep thought for about ten minutes while I let the class get a drink and go to the bathroom. Once they were all seated, I smiled and announced that we were going to learn about angles. I wrote "acute," "right," and "obtuse" on the board. I asked them if they knew (or remembered) what these angles were. They all pretty much kept a blank, uninterested look on their faces, and there was silence. I told them to leave their math books in their desks and to just do what I did. I then raised my right hand next to my face with my thumb pointing straight out toward my mouth and my index finger about 45 degrees from my thumb. I folded the rest of my fingers. They all followed suit. "This," I announced in a sweet little voice, "is an acute angle. Isn't it cute? It's so little and tiny and adorable." They looked at me, wondering if I had indulged in a liquid lunch. But, still pleased their books were in their desks, they all repeated the angle using little voices.

Once we practiced it a few times, I introduced the obtuse angle. Keeping my thumb where it was, I moved my index finger to about 130 degrees. With a low, deep voice I announced, "This is an obtuse angle. He's big and massive. You can even hear it in the letter sounds and the way you move your mouth: big, round letters." I then said the word slowly and accentuated the vowel sounds, making my mouth look very round and large. They all were getting into it now, realizing that I was doing this as a "learning joke" and they could smile, get silly, and even laugh.

We then went back and forth, moving from acute to obtuse, using the voices and going faster and faster. It was time for the right angle. I left my thumb where it was and moved my index finger to point straight up in the air. "This—" I paused as they mimicked the motion— "is the right angle. It's called that because it is right in the middle of acute and obtuse. Right smack dab in the middle." (Okay, I understand that there are mathematicians who would argue with me, but let's focus on the audience and cut a little slack.) I gave my right angle information in a natural voice. I then explained that anything smaller than the right angle was acute and anything larger than the right angle was obtuse. The right angle was always just right in the middle. It was beginning to sound a little like *Goldilocks and the Three Angles*.

We played around with this for about five more minutes, introducing the number of degrees for the right angle and straight line. We wrote degrees on the board and made the sizes of the angles with our hands and said the words with the correlating voices. We were done in less than fifteen minutes. Everyone knew their angles. The rest of the time, we talked about how to learn and about what makes us remember things, and we did some magic with the number nine. The good thing about being a sub is that usually, no one is bent out of shape if you depart from the text or close the book altogether as long as the kids learn the information. Isn't that the way it should be all the time?

A few months later, I was subbing for another room and passed the "angles" class in the hall. A group of students said hi, started laughing, and began to make the hand angles, reciting the names and using their "angle voices." I smiled, so pleased that they remembered. I gave them a thumbs-up and silently prayed they didn't say the angles that way in regular math class. Next time I'll have to tell them it's our little secret.

The Middle School Math

One day in fall during my retirement years, I was at the administration building where the math coordinator had called me into his office. I was a bit surprised that he wanted to see me, of all people, and then was completely shocked when he stated that he had been told I would be a good candidate to help the seventh graders prepare for the math part of the mastery testing. I have no idea who gave him this erroneous information. As far as I was concerned, an algebraic expression was some common colloquial phrase used in the obscure country of Algebrai. I smiled though, and not wanting to diminish his stellar opinion of me, I said "Sure, sounds great!"

Luckily, there *were* a few things that were great about it. I was blessed, yet again, to be working with a fantastic math teacher, who by the grace of some wise administrator had an extra teacher's manual for me to use. Teacher's manuals are the Gutenberg Bible of middle-school academia. They are very rare and seldom shared. She also, in her infinite wisdom, had worked out a plan where she would teach the first part of the class and in the second part we would go around and help individual students who were either completely apathetic or confused or a little bit of both.

Once again, as in college chemistry, I was her best student. I took notes as she spoke and followed along in the manual. I even did the homework at night and then checked my answers with the manual. I could probably have passed the course with a C-. I did have two things going for me. I was an adult now, and if I had the answer I could usually figure out by process of elimination how to get there. The other thing I had going for me was that I understood exactly how those confused students felt, with a bit of sympathy left over for the apathetic.

The Apathetic

One of my more secure lessons was the one on percentages. I had that one pretty much under my belt as I went around helping the students. One girl hadn't even made an attempt at the examples. I asked her if she wanted some help. Her answer was a rather snippy no, due to the fact, she told me, that she would never need percentages, so why bother knowing them. "Never need percentages?" I responded, adding, "Don't you like to shop?" Now I had her interest. Yes, she loved to shop. Well, duh, percentages were the key to shopping. "I mean," I continued, "what if your favorite jeans are on sale at 40 percent off? Wouldn't you want to know if you could afford to buy two pair instead of one?" She gave this some thought, looked down at her paper, then back at me and asked, "So, how do I do this..."

When all else fails, shopping can arouse a keen sense of interest.

The Confused

I was great when working with the confused student. For one thing, I felt better that there was someone else in the room more confused than I was. For another, I was always so patient and understanding. I had been there. I had done that. I had a closet full of "Say What? I'm confused," t-shirts. I was working with kindred spirits.

At one lesson, I was yet again besieged by those horrific equations that recruited letters and gave them the status of numbers. This poor girl was sitting at her desk staring blankly at the equation, as if willing it to go away. I went over and offered my help. She said I could try, and added "I'll never get this." I looked down at the paper to the first equation. It read something like "2x + 3y = 6y." The teacher's manual was easy enough to follow: the "3y" had to go on the other side and the sign had to be changed. Why this had to happen, I had no idea. I took the only course left to me. I would make something up and I would have it relate to her.

"So," I began, "think of this as a Friday night school dance. All the *x*'s are the girls and all the *y*'s are the boys." (At least I could do science a favor and keep it fairly chromosomally correct.) I asked the student if she could picture herself at the dance. What was she wearing? She gave a pretty detailed description, so I knew she was on her way to chasing the fear factor out of the dance. I told her that her best friend was with her and asked her name and what she had on. By this point, she was completely animated and relieved that she was escaping math.

This is where the hook comes in. The boy that she really likes (who she didn't have to name) is standing just five feet away from her and she can tell that he wants to ask her to dance. But the thing about the dance was that it couldn't start until all the girls were on one side of the room and all the boys were on the opposite side. There's always a catch.

I then had her picture the math equation as the dance. All the *x*'s, or girls, go on one side and all the *y*'s, or boys, on the other. To get the *y*'s, or the boy she wants to dance with, to the opposite side where he belonged with the other *y*'s, he had to go across the middle of the room—the equal sign. Also very important: when he and the other boys went to the opposite side of the equal sign (the room), the sign they had before them had to change, to none other than the opposite sign—ergo, the plus becomes a minus, a minus becomes a plus, a times sign becomes a division sign and a division sign becomes a times. (There was a song here somewhere, I just knew it.) The point is that a lot of repeating of the word "opposite" is good for memory, and I always throw in some big hand gestures over moving them from one side to another. It's a kinesthetic thing.

I was hoping that I had made myself clear and watched as she looked down at the example and started doing it. She got it. She was thrilled. The fear was gone. One girl sitting near her asked if I would help her. I didn't have a chance to answer. My new math protégée said she would do it. "It's so easy," she told the girl, and brought her to the dance.

I'm sure there's a law against teaching math that way, but I truly believe that along with some other areas, all's fair in love, war, and algebraorithm. There's nothing wrong, either, with a student feeling good about herself in math for once. Believe me, I know.

If you want to skip the dance, you can move the x's *and* y's *over to sports and have teams, or just pick whatever you think might work.*

The Movies and the Math Lesson

This was an out-of-school experience, but it raised some questions and offered a confirmation. I went to the movies one night with a friend. I had rushed to get there and skipped dinner, so I headed for the junk food at the concession stand. I chose the least junkiest (I know that's not a word) of choices and ordered from the kid behind the counter. He informed me that he could not sell me anything unless I had the exact change because the change bar on the computerized cash register was down. I didn't have the exact change. Well, I can get pretty ugly when I'm starving, and I wasn't going to let modern mechanical glitches get in the way of me and my food. I told him to just make the change himself. "I can't do that," he replied, obviously shocked that I would even ask.

"Oh, yes you can," I answered. "Just count up." I then walked him through the process. I had a ten dollar bill. The item was $4.46. How much more did he need to get to $4.50? He answered four cents. "So give me the four cents," I requested, which he did. Now, at $4.50, how much more would he need to get to $5.00? He answered fifty cents, which I also took from him. We were on our way. And the final question was, how much more to get to $10.00? He got it—$5.00, which he also handed me, along with my junk food.

He was thrilled, maybe even in complete awe. I don't remember, I was too busy unwrapping my dinner. He asked me to stay for the next customer to see if he could do it again. I said sure, no problem. He did a fine job, too, and I gave him a thumbs-up. The manager, looking a bit out of sorts, came rushing over and wanted to know why he was disobeying orders and making change. His answer was simple and full of pride: "Because I know how." And proved it by teaching his boss how to count up. The kid had everything under control. My work was done and so was my junk food, so I moved on to the movie. In hindsight, I should have gotten the food for free, first of all because no one should have to actually pay for that stuff and second, because I thought I earned it.

I'm sure that the cashier, like the rest of us, had learned that process somewhere in school. I certainly don't remember my first go-round. I do remember relearning it, though, when I had a part-time job as a cashier at a sporting goods store before cash registers had computerized brains. I actually had to figure it out myself, just imagine! I was taught by a girl who probably didn't even finish high school. I guess she was a better teacher than the one I had in school. Or maybe my teacher should have had a "why you should teach this" manual along with a "this is what you have to teach" manual. Maybe the course should have been called Practical Math Experiences.

On page one of the manual would be the lesson "How to count up in case your computer breaks on the cash register of the future and you have to make change for people buying junk food at the movies."

22
Chemistry

When the Atom Didn't Bomb

One of my life's most ironic moments was when I was subbing long term for an eighth-grade self-contained special-ed class. The students went out to the regular classes for social studies and, yes, chemistry. This meant I couldn't ignore it. I not only had to teach it, I had to learn it! Luckily, I was team teaching with a clone of my previous chemistry teacher and I finally began to think there was hope for me in the sciences. Perhaps not much, but just a little spark of recognition.

A test on the atom was coming up. I stood at the front of my room pretending that I was ready to review with my class. The blackboard behind me was empty and the faces of my students looked just as empty, and I'm sure I mirrored their expressions. I had to think quickly and come up with a stupendous wing-it program. Two things were needed. One, get them interested in atoms. Two, get them to relate to atoms.

I prayed to my muse of inspirational fire and started talking. I told them that everything—every single, little, minute thing up to every humongous thing on this earth and stretching out to the universe—was made up of atoms, including us. There were billions and billions of atoms right in the room with us, surrounding us, inside of us, our skin, our stomachs, our eyelashes, our fingernails, teeth, toes, and if we still had them, our tonsils. Not only that, but we lived on recycled atoms. We were made up of the same things as everything on this earth and even the stars that we wished upon. We could have parts of infamous or famous people in us. We could share the parts of trees, slugs, earthworms, dogs, giraffes, ants or elephants. You name it; we could have been part of it. Pretty soon, we are all staring at our arms, hands, and hair and wondering who or what we once shared all our parts with. We even talked a little about what or who we would like or not like to be a part of our physical makeup.

Now the atom interest was there, so I went onto part two: getting the class to relate to atoms so they would remember the information. I decided to stick to a good thing: "streets and houses" with a few modifications, including a huge extension of the area being "mapped." I drew a circle on the board. "This is the world, and it's also the shape of the atom," I said. Now, rumor has it that in fact it is not the shape of the atom. We weren't going for realism, we were going for getting it right on the test, and the circle was what the test and the CT Mastery wanted. And that's what they were going to get, come hell or high water.

Once the circle or atom was drawn, I put a house in the center. I told the class that in the world of atoms, there lived three inhabitants. There were the protons, the electrons, and the neutrons. To help them remember the three, I pointed out that they all rhyme at the end. As a clue, I wrote the word P-E-N on the board: *P* for protons, *E* for electrons, and *N* for neutrons. For once, a useful acronym!

"So," I asked, "where do they live on planet Atom?" This was a rhetorical question so I continued talking. I told them that the protons and the neutrons live together in the house, and that in the world of atoms, the house is called a nucleus. And the electrons live outside the house. To help support this last point, I told them that "electron" begins the same way as "electricity." Electricity gives us light like the sun does, and the sun in any drawing goes outside the house. I had them practice drawing it, writing it down, and even let some of them come to the board and repeat the process in front of the class.

The day of the test came. My students, gratefully, had the modified test and were only responsible for basic information about the atom. It was a nail-biting experience for me as I watched them take the test. Later, the science teacher found me during my free period. She was smiling and said all my students had passed with an A grade. Then she showed me the tests. There was the circle of the atom. Inside each one was a neat little house; some even had chimneys or a lovely little tree. Outside was a sun shining on the house, but *electron* was written in the sun, and those protons and neutrons were happily nestled together in home sweet home.

I thanked the teacher for being so generous with what to count as correct. She said she was happy to do that, and she added, "Well, I'm sure they're never going to be teaching chemistry." I nodded in agreement and chose to omit telling her of the time that statement was once said of me. Before leaving, she said she was curious about one thing. Why had they all written P-E-N at the tops of their papers? I hadn't noticed that when first looking at the papers, being so impressed with the atomic artwork. I explained that it was an acronym clue to remember the "-ons." She said she loved the idea and asked if she could use it in the future with her classes. I answered that of course she could. After all, anything I can do to help teach chemistry…

23
Behavior

Check This Out (the extended version)

Check marks have become the villain throughout our educational careers. "If you do that again, you'll get a check!" I remember so many teachers threaten this over and over in every grade, and they weren't talking about the kind of check you cash at the bank. It's those two connecting, angled lines, one short, one long. Consequently, a check mark, a purely innocent written sign, got a bad rap. I decided to change that. It was time for it to be liberated from its austere, preposterous, bogus, cynical history. Why should a plus sign have all the popularity, smiles, and fun?

It is amazing how putting a check mark on the board or piece of paper can work some kind of serene magic. It's doesn't cost anything, it's not a prize, but in its own way somehow, these two small lines are this great motivator to challenge and conquer the negative. Maybe it just lets students know that you're checking out how well they're doing. I never get tired of using it. I've tried it from grade school to middle school and begged a teacher to death until she tried it in high school. It's not perfect or even foolproof, but it's free, you don't have to study it, take a course in it, or even pack it in a bag. You just have to remember to focus on the positive, comment on it, and put a check on a board. How easy is that!

I started using the checks when I was an inclusion teacher. I tried it for behavior and for academics, anything a group or child needed. In a small group, each child got checks for success and the competition was only with themselves, not with anyone else. I called it "beat your own score." If the kids read more words correctly in each list of speed drills, they got checks. If they answered more math problems correctly, they got checks. They just had to do better in whatever they needed to do better in. It was that simple. The beauty of it was, from a facilitator-of-mandates's point of view, it was a great way to document. If asked if a child is improving, you can say something like "Yes, he got six more checks than yesterday." (Okay, I don't think it would really fly, but it's a thought.)

The substitute

It was actually when I started subbing that I found the true beauty in the check system. So, let me introduce, to anyone who has ever subbed, your new best friend: Mr. Check. Let's say you walk into a third-grade class as a sub. Actually, you could be walking into anywhere from first on up, but let's just say it's third. I picked this grade because it's at the midpoint of the language modifications you can use. In lower grades you can scale down a bit; in higher grades scale it up a bit. There is a method to this madness.

As the students pile in, write "row 1, row 2, row 3" and so forth on the board in rows going down, for however many rows of seats are in the classroom. This usually gets some of the students' attention. With the attention comes some curiosity, and with that comes anticipation about what you are up to—ergo, behavior can become quieter and more cautious. Some kids will ask what the list is for and just tell them you'll let them know when everyone is seated. This can give you a bit of an upper hand, depending on the class. (Remember, there are some individuals and even some groups who need something more like a siren, bells, and whistles to get their attention. I recommend for this type of situation that you feign being ill and just go home, or at least try to.)

Once everyone is seated, introduce yourself and write your name on the board. If you have a last name like mine, I suggest having the students call you by the initial of your last name. Most kids just call me "Miss I." I then point to a row, any row, when it looks like they are listening and I comment on their outstanding behavior. I name a few of those behaviors and give them a check.

Then you recite the rules. Rules are your choice. Me? I like everyone to raise their hands before they get out of their seats, just so I know where they are going. I like it quiet, the old "eyes up here," and well, you know the drill.

Each row gets a check for good behavior, and one row is very happy because they already got two and morning announcements haven't even started yet. A hand will go up and someone will ask what they get for those checks. That never fails. I tell them it earns them rights. The right to go get a drink, the right to sharpen their pencils, the right to line up first to leave the room, the right for free time at the end of the day...whatever floats the boat of peace and tranquility. If someone makes a mistake and doesn't follow the rules, his or her row can lose a check. When mistakes are made, I tell them I have to correct that behavior or I have to take away a check. All they have to do to keep it is say they are sorry and stop the behavior, and we all move on. That helps eliminate a day full of vendettas.

Usually as you are going through all this they sit quietly, so I tell them they all earned a check. They like that, they're up one more, and you're keeping your end of the bargain. Never underestimate the wonders of immediate gratification. If a child who is sitting in, say, row 2 starts talking, don't say anything to him; just announce that all the other rows are getting a check for working so quietly. The other kids in row 2 will give the one talking a dirty look or a "Shhhh," and now he looks bad and you don't. You are not the enemy and that is a good place to be. If a child asks to get a drink, look up at the rows of check marks like you are studying it. If that row is doing well, say something like, "Yes, your row is doing well." If there a lot fewer check marks there, say something like, "Well, your row isn't doing too well right now. Let's give it a few minutes and see if you can get some more checks so you can go."

I give lots of checks. If they are working quietly, I go up to the board without saying anything and put a few checks in each row. Some kids look up and they get a big smile from me. They get checks for right answers and even good wrong answers. They get checks for saying "please" or "thank you," for sharing, for helping out, lining up without pushing, whatever they do that is positive gets a check.

Before lunch, I count up the checks, erase them, and write down the totals in numerals. Then I start marking that afternoon's checks. When there's about a half hour left in the day, we count up the checks from the afternoon and add them to the morning's number. Usually, all the rows have earned their free time. With this comes a day's end when you are happy, they are happy, and everyone leaves for the day happily ever after.

Yes, in my dreams and most fairy tales, but if you want to, check it out. See what happens. If it doesn't work, then erase the checks from the board and maybe try using circles. Or, just maybe, you are one of those amazing teachers I've seen who just holds a class's attention and behavior by your mere presence. I can't do that. If you can't either, maybe this will help. I hope so.

Go to the Stick

This is a true story. I couldn't make it make it up, Scout's honor. While still a resource teacher, I was working with a number of students in one of the second-grade classes. The teacher was top-notch, but this class tended to be incredibly chatty. I figured that if she couldn't get them to stop talking, the only thing left to do was to reach into the creative bag of tricks. I decided to borrow the "talking stick" idea from the Native Americans.

I got a twelve-inch wooden dowel. I painted some Native American-looking symbols around it. At the top I tied a string with feathers and shells hanging. The class was sitting in a circle for "morning meeting." I told the class the story of the talking stick and how the only person who could be talking was the one who held the stick. I embellished a bit, of course, because kids like a story. They liked the idea, and the class began to grasp the concept of polite listening skills. (Actually, a pointer can work just as well if you're not into woodworking or artwork.)

There was one poor boy who was still having issues. He was a nice kid, really, but every once in a while he would start yelling out, throwing things, and become overwhelmingly defiant. After a scene, he would cry and apologize profusely. It was time for desperately ingenious measures. I used the stick. No, I didn't hit him. I did ask him if he knew when one of these episodes was coming on. He said that in fact, he did. He would start to feel tense and angry, and it would just take control of him. Not to worry, I told him, we wanted to help him get rid of this behavior. And I began to make up an elaborate story about the stick.

When he felt this anger coming on, he was to get up, get the stick, and go to the back of the room. The classroom teacher was with us; she gave him the smile and nod that this was okay with her. We then got the stick and went to the back of the room.

I told him there was a certain procedure we had to follow. I knelt down on the floor and showed him how to lean back, resting his upper body on his legs and heels. He did the same. I then showed him how to stretch out his arms and had him hold the stick with both hands. He was taking all this very seriously, which was a good sign.

The next part was the most important. He was to close his eyes and breathe very deeply. We practiced this a few times. Once the breathing was going well, he was to picture all that dark anger in his head and surround it with light. Still breathing, he was to pass that anger from his head, down his neck, and let it divide. Half was to pass down through one arm and the other half down the other arm. Once it got to his hands, he was to give his anger to the stick. The stick would take it and shoot it right out the top, right out of the room and far into the sky where it would break up into millions of pieces and lose all its power.

I was so thankful for all those yoga classes I took. All those deep breathing and visualization skills were put to use for a second grader. All he needed was a prop to get it to work. Work it did. The teacher said he was doing so much better, and he was so happy that he wasn't falling prey to the dark side.

Was I telling him a lie about the power of the stick? It's pretty much along similar lines as what I said to the boy with the talking goblins. Did the boy really believe the stick had this power? He believed that he really didn't want to get angry. He believed that this was helping him. Beliefs are a gray area, and I'm cheering for his because *I* believe he found a way to conquer what he needed to conquer. He probably gave the stick up long ago, but I'll bet he's still breathing deeply and visualizing that anger right out the door.

I have to admit that I sometimes wonder how much he or the other kids in class bought the story or whether they just decided to go along with it for its novelty. I do know that after they saw how he was doing so much better, once in a while one of the other students would raise a hand and ask the teacher if he or she could "go to the stick." Well, I guess the motto here is "If it works, stick to it."

I do suggest though that if a student is prone to bouts of violent behavior, you make the stick out of a paper towel roll just in case it *doesn't* work.

Bees with Honey

You know that old annoying, roll-your-eyes saying: "If you don't have something nice to say, don't say anything at all." It actually has a place here. If a student is talking in class when he or she shouldn't be, mum's the word to that child, but pick the student closest to the talker who is actually focused on the lesson and say, loud enough for the talker to hear, "I like the way you're listening." You can even give the listening student some type of reward, like an extra check or a trip to the water fountain.

When the student who was talking finally stops, make it a point to walk by the desk and comment on the child's good behavior. It's not easy, I know. Just say what you really want to say in your head and make sure it's not what's coming out of your mouth. Every once in a while, pay a student a compliment out of the blue, just for the heck of it. Look for the "yes" responses, not the "no's." The positive can help eradicate the negative. It's that glass-half-full-or-half-empty mind-set. I should state that if you are the regular classroom teacher you can shorten the amount of comments considerably as the year goes on. Eventually a smile can pretty much say it all.

If you're in the room and the students are lined up outside the door, look at the first four standing there and say something like "Perfect! You may pass in." Stop the rest and repeat the comment. This helps to let them know that you are in charge here, but also that you're not an ogre. If you can know ahead of time who is the worst kid in the room, I'd say start off the positive comments with that one. Try to use words like "perfect," "excellent," "absolutely," "exactly." When you get home after all this exhausting niceness, I suggest you pick an inanimate object (say, the refrigerator) and start yelling your head off. Only use obscenities if absolutely necessary.

CONCLUSION

So, let me just say, since you have made it to the end of the book: "Perfect, fantastic, great job, excellent!" I just hope no one is standing in front of the fridge swearing away, regretting the read.

Just remember that learning, like food and clothes, is essential to living. One size does not fit all, and everyone's tastes and amount of consumption varies. They do say that variety is the spice of life, so maybe we need to spice up education a bit more. If you need some time to digest all this information, then I would say to just put on some Gregorian chants, strike a Zen pose, breathe deeply, empty your head, let go of the fear factor, and repeat the mantra:

Teach them; they can learn.
Teach them how to learn.
Teach them to love learning.
The test score is not the cause of my teaching. The test score is the effect of my teaching.
I love to teach what I love.
All's well that's ends well, as long as it ends in a circle.

I think Shakespeare forgot to add that last little bit.

A FEW GREAT BOOKS

Charney, Ruth Sidney. *Teaching Children to Care*. Northeast Foundation for Children, 1992.

Unger, Harlow Giles. *Noah Webster: The Life and Times of an American Patriot.* John Wiley & Sons, Inc., 1998.

Kendall, Joshua. The Forgotten Founding Father, G.P. Putnam's Sons New York, 2010.

And any edition of the works of Shakespeare (complete or in part), if you are so inspired.

ACKNOWLEDGMENTS

Jill Rubalcaba is a fantastic writer of children's and young adult books and is just as fantastic for giving her time and interest to guide, edit, and support my writing.

To Ari Iaccarino, Cindy Beauchamp, Bernadette Cappella, Vinny Cervoni, Leslie Dockendorff, Carol Donzella, Jan Doyle, Pam Hirth, Mary Howland, Ellen Hovercamp, Sue Hunt, Guy Iaccarino, Sherry Kaufman Iaccarino, Ron Imbriglio, Nancy Paone, Kathy Frumento, Lori Maltese, Createspace team 4 and all the other saving graces I've mentioned: thank you.

Made in the USA
Columbia, SC
16 October 2018